THE BOOK OF RATINGS

THE BOOK OF
RATINGS

OPINIONS, GRADES, AND ASSESSMENTS OF EVERYTHING WORTH THINKING ABOUT

Lore Fitzgerald Sjöberg

ILLUSTRATIONS BY STEPHEN NOTLEY

THREE RIVERS PRESS · NEW YORK

Published by Three Rivers Press, New York, New York.
Member of the Crown Publishing Group,
a division of Random House, Inc.
www.randomhouse.com

THREE RIVERS PRESS and the Tugboat design are
registered trademarks of Random House, Inc.

Portions of this work were previously published on
www.brunching.com.

Printed in the United States of America

DESIGN BY KAREN MINSTER

Library of Congress Cataloging-in-Publication Data

The Book of ratings : opinions, grades, and assessments of
everything worth thinking about / edited by L. Fitzgerald
Sjöberg, illustrations by Stephen Notley.—1st ed.
1. Life—Humor.   2. American wit and humor.
I. Sjöberg, L. Fitzgerald (Lore Fitzgerald)
II. Notley, Stephen

PN6231.L48 R38 2002
818'.60208—dc21   2002019405

ISBN 0-609-80852-4

10 9 8 7 6 5 4 3 2 1

First Edition

This book is dedicated to Colette.

CONTENTS

ACKNOWLEDGMENTS

MANY AND VARIED THANKS TO

David and Ann Neilsen, the Spinnwebe Ruffiani,
my old housemates at the Marshmallow Peanut Circus,
the Order of the Individual Cereal Unit, Lori Matsumoto,
Amity Warren and Lorie Hull, Carmel Adelberg,
Eric Lipton, Steve Connelly, Craig Demel,
Steve Berlin-Chavez, Don Hochstein, Mr. Pants,
Nutas McGrootas, Larry Wall, Linus Torvalds,
and everyone involved in my conception,
gestation, and birth.

INTRODUCTION

THE RATINGS ARE THE RESULT OF A PATHOLOGICAL, ALMOST erotic urge to provide a service sorely lacking in modern society. While the common citizen has no end of self-proclaimed and self-cleaning experts to consult on such weighty matters as what movie to see, what music to buy, and what local theater production to pretend to have attended, for some reason no such assistance is provided when considering what sugar-bonded breakfast cereal to eat, what pizza topping to order, or what dinosaur to, you know, enjoy. Appreciate. Something like that.

Having identified this unstuffed niche, I leapt boldly and metaphorically into action, writing the first few Ratings and then pretty much just sitting on them until Dave Neilsen—my sometime collaborator, oldest friend, and iridologist—invited me to join him in an exciting new opportunity in mass communication: vanity radio. When that ended up being even more of a ripoff than we had anticipated, we quit. And that was pretty much it until the whole Web thing happened.

The Web, as future scholars will no doubt acknowledge, holds the distinction of being the only form of mass communication in which you can reach out to kindred spirits around the globe, changing lives and being changed in turn, while still pretending that you're working on a spreadsheet when the boss walks by. Try *that* with ham radio. As such, it was the perfect medium for the musings of the reincarnated Brunching Shuttlecocks, which, like a ninja or a craving for chicken tenders, can strike at any time.

Today, the Ratings are read by dozens—perhaps hundreds of thousands of dozens—of people around the world.

Even more excitingly, if science fiction anthologies are to believed, electronic emissions containing the Ratings reached Alpha Centauri a year or so ago, where the massively intelligent and multibreasted denizens of that system should be wishing they had some Oreo O's even now.

THE BOOK OF RATINGS

HOSTESS PRODUCTS

Twinkies

The quintessential Hostess food, superficially similar to foods you might create in your own kitchen, yet profoundly different. Yes, the outer layer bears a passing resemblance to sponge cake, and the "creamy filling" might have once read a book about a dairy product, but overall it has that quality of taste and texture that can only be found in the snack food aisle. **A+**

Cup Cakes

What is it with the so-called frosting? It's this weird flat tortilla of sugar and chocolate clinging pathetically to the much larger cake unit. The best theory I've heard is that the cake and frosting of a Hostess Cup Cake are actually the male and female versions of the same species, locked in chocolatey symbiosis. This would mean that the little swirl of white frosting on top is actually genetic material, which, let's face it, is what it resembles in the first place. **B+**

Chocodiles

Rebel Twinkies. Chocodiles reject the hypocritical sociability of the other Twinkies in their happy little packs of three, wrapped in plastic and denial, and instead choose to go it alone, sitting in their chocolatey leather jackets and brooding about the futility of existence. But they're hard to find and really not as tasty, so they get a **B.**

Fruit Pies

Hostess is the reigning monarch of handheld pies. You can keep your Dolly Madison, your Home Run pies, your miniature pecan pie gas station desserts: Give me a cherry Hostess Fruit Pie and a place to eat it and I shall gain some weight. Other manufacturers skimp on the fruit filling, the shortening for the crust, the festive artificial coloring, but not Hostess. Truly the luxury model. **A**

Suzy Qs

What is the point? Do we really need a Hostess product where you can see the "creamy filling" before you even open the package? The end result is that a thick layer of the dessert in question remains attached to the wrapper, not to mention the fact that the filling is free to squeege out all over your fingers if you're not careful. Not the sort of snack food I want my children exposed to. **C–**

Ding Dongs and Ho Hos

Unfortunately, I have reached an impasse on perhaps the most controversial issue of our time: Which are better, Ding Dongs or Ho Hos? Blood is shed daily on the streets of some of our more pathetic cities over this very question, and I have a friend who has promised to personally whack me with a titanium microphone stand if I come out on the wrong side, although I've forgotten which she prefers. Well, what the hell, let's say serve Ho Hos with red meat and Ding Dongs with fish and give them both an **A.**

STUFF IN THE
AIRLINE CATALOG

EVAC-U8 Emergency Escape Smoke Hood

This would be hard to explain to a child. There should be an accompanying video entitled *Sometimes It's Okay to Put a Bag Over Your Head* with a patient explanation of the difference between an emergency smoke hood and a Kroger produce bag. Other uses: playing "Darth Vader's Laundry Day," hotboxing. **C–**

Remote Wireless Meat Themometer

"Monitor meat's temperature without leaving your armchair." To this day, scholars cannot determine how the pyramids were built without the ability to tell what temperature meat is without having to get right up close to it. The best theory right now is aliens with meat beams, but there are those who feel that the ancient Egyptians must have had some sort of primitive wireless meat thermometer made out of birds. **C–**

Ionic Breeze Personal Air Purifier

Also known as the "I Am an Uptight Asshole Medallion." It blows "cleaner air" up your nose so that you can have the higher-quality atmosphere the lower classes just haven't earned. What I want to see, what I would dearly love to see, is some guy trying to pick up someone in a bar while wearing this. "It blows clean air, baby. That's right, ionized. Oh, yeah." **D–**

Authentic Pachinko Game

I'm just glad it's authentic, because once I ordered a pachinko game and I forgot to check the "authentic" box and they sent me one of those little Cracker Jack toys where you have to get the little BBs on the puppy's eyes, and it lacked that authentic pachinko experience that I was hoping for. **B+**

Remote-Controlled Indoor Triple-Turbo Blimp

Okay, so you have a remote-controlled indoor blimp for sale, and some people will dig on that. And if you point out that it's a turbo blimp, that's going to entice a few more fence-sitters. But then there's that reluctant demographic that's been looking at the double-turbo blimps for years now and almost buying them, maybe even pulling out the credit card, but deciding against it at the last minute. And that's where this hot little number comes in. **B**

The World's Largest Crossword Puzzle

I like that the ad specifies that there are no repeat clues, because I never even would have considered the possibility that all the clues could just be "The noise a smoke alarm makes." Thanks, Hammacher Schlemmer! **C+**

DEADLY SINS

Sloth

I'm big on sloth. Sloth is cheap and easy to get. You need a partner or at least an object to get the most out of lust; gluttony and avarice both take something of a financial investment; but sloth is damned convenient. You can get in some quality sloth in your own bedroom, watching TV or even at the office. And if anyone gives you a hard time about it, just point out that by doing nothing, you're helping to slow down the endless march of entropy and delay the eventual heat death of the universe. **B+**

Gluttony

Most people group sloth and gluttony together as the "slob sins," but the fact is that your dedicated glutton puts a lot of effort into his or her sin. Finding the stores with the pillowcase-sized bags of potato chips, checking out which lunch buffets shut down at two o'clock and which go on until three-thirty, taping Nabisco commercials—gluttony can be hard work. Take time out to give a glutton you know a pat on the back and a bite of your sandwich, just to say, "Hey, thanks for being a glutton." **C+**

Wrath

Lousy sin. Unsociable, bad on the nerves, and drives property values down. And what do you have to show for it? An ulcer and bruised knuckles, that's what. And it's so vulgar. Take it from me, pass on the wrath. Not only will you be less damned, you'll be happier. **D**

Lust

Ah, lust. Putting the "deadly" back into the seven deadly sins. The nasty thing is that while you need to trade liquids to get dead from lust, all you have to do to be damned to eternal hellfire and torment is lust in your heart. Talk about adding insult to injury. I lust in my heart all the time— heart, brain, endocrine glands, the whole shebang. Even if I *wanted* to not lust, I'm not sure how I'd go about it. Still, of all the deadly sins, this one is its own reward. **B**

Pride

I'm not sure how this one works. Is plain old everyday pride sinful or do you have to get into the realm of hubris before you're in trouble? Do you go to hell for saying, "This is a pretty tasty three-bean salad I've made, if I do say so myself," or do you have to say, "Why, I bet this is a better three-bean salad than *God* could make"? And what about self-esteem? My high school counselors were always pushing self-esteem on me. Were they pawns of the Adversary? So many questions. **C**

Envy

This is another of those thinking sins. Do you get damned for *thinking* about another slice of pie? Do you burn for *considering* hitting the snooze alarm? No, of course not, but all you have to do is covet something of someone else and boom, you're a brimstone hors d'oeuvre. You don't have to lay a *hand* on your neighbor's manservant to get the ecclesiastical zot. There should really be some sort of appeals process. **C–**

Avarice

Also known as greed. Got a lot of good press in the eighties. Still has a lot of supporters. If gluttony were as popular as greed, the snack food industry would own us all like so much stacked firewood. The problem with avarice is that it gets pretty ludicrous pretty quickly. From billionaires buying a dozen gold Cadillacs to bozos gushing over costume jewelry on the Home Shopping Network, greedy people inevitably end up looking goofy in public. **D**

DINOSAURS

Brontosaurus

Huge beast. Ate only plants, but could crush a '93 Cabriolet with a single step of its titanic brontosaurus feet. Name means "thunder lizard," which is about as cool as you can get. Its only real drawback is that it didn't really exist. **B+**

Apatosaurus

This is what they're calling brontosauruses these days. Apparently, they had some problem with the wrong skull on the wrong body—duh—and once they figured it out, they had to change the name to "apatosaurus," which means "deceptive lizard." Personally, I think they should have looked up the Latin for "stupid scientist." **D**

Dimetrodon

Looks like a gecko with a mohawk. Big sail on its back that they think attracted mates or conserved body heat. Actually, that's what scientists say about anything on an animal they don't understand. They could find evidence of an iguanadon with a ZZ Top beard and they'd say "the beard was probably to conserve body heat or attract mates." Which, come to think of it, is probably what ZZ Top uses them for. Anyhow, **C.**

Tyrannosaurus Rex

Cool animal. Name means "tyrant lizard king." Cool. I wish my name meant "tyrant lizard king." Anyhow, we all know what makes this such a great dinosaur—it could completely eat you. Plus the little tiny forearms make it look like some demented nightmare beast from the fertile mind of Tim Burton. **A+**

Velociraptor

These guys got a lot of press from *Jurassic Park,* but let's face it, they're pretty lacking. They couldn't even manage to eat two little kids, one of whom had only minutes before been turned into a toaster pastry. Sure, they got the hunter, but he was coming up with cute last words when he should have been running like a bunny. And then all three of them got totally worked by a baby tyrannosaurus! Lame! **D!**

Stegosaurus

Two words: spiked tail. "Oh, so you're sneaking up behind me to eat my delicious body? *Wham!* Spikes! For you! In your head!" Plus it had I-am-an-industrial-monster plates on its back, which, while probably for conserving body heat or attracting mates, were impressive-looking. **A**

MIRACLES OF CHRIST

Money in a Fish

Needless to say, the ability to find money in fish is not one of Christ's more well-advertised miracles. To begin with, coming up with cash money sounds insufficiently Christlike. "Arise, my child, for you are healed" sounds like something Jesus would say. "Hey, look, a quarter!" does not. Secondly, the whole thing is just a little too "News of the Weird." **D**

Driving Out Demons

This is a good one. Jesus comes across a guy who is possessed by not one but bunches of demons, which I imagine feels something like scabies, only with the smell of brimstone and a much deeper voice to go along with it. For some reason the demons, realizing their infernal number is up, beg to be sent into a nearby herd of pigs. So Christ complies and the pigs— all two thousand of them—charge down and drown themselves in a lake. I'm sure it's all very symbolic. **C+**

Water into Wine

According to John, this is the first miracle the Son of God performed, and I have to say it's a good one to start the show with. It's impressive, it's elegant, and it carries more obvious benefit than, say, changing a beet into a rutabaga.

And He performed it for the benefit of guests at a wedding, which shows that God loves even those too lamebrained to call a caterer. **A+**

Healing en Masse

"[T]he multitude wondered, when they saw the dumb to speak, the maimed to be whole, the lame to walk, and the blind to see. [Matt. 15:31]" This is an important miracle because it shows that Christ has organizational skills. A lesser messiah might have gotten all confused in the turmoil, and then the multitude would have witnessed the crippled seeing, the blind walking, the dumb made whole, and the maimed speaking, and then the wondering would have been more along the lines of "What the hey?" **B+**

Walking on Water

It's interesting to me that so many of Christ's non-healing-oriented miracles involved water, fish, or both. Water into wine, fishes and loaves, walking on water, the aforementioned money in a fish, and so forth. But it's probably just as well that all this miracle-working took place by the shore in the Middle East, because not only is the ability to walk on tundra much less impressive, but it would look pretty silly to have the faithful attaching little outlines of caribou to their cars. **A−**

Withering a Fig Tree

You might want to look this one up, because if you haven't read it, you're not going to believe me. It's in Matthew 21:18–22. Christ is hungry, he sees a fig tree, but there are no figs, so in a scene reminiscent of "The Fox and the Grapes II: The Revenge," he curses the tree so that it will never grow fruit again. Weird. Eerie. Disturbing. **C−**

MYTHICAL CREATURES

Dragons

The problem with dragons is that you only hear about them when they get killed, thus leaving the impression that dragons are huge, fire-breathing, enormously destructive creatures that are really quite easy to take down. They need to add more background material to dragon stories, along the lines of "Chapter 14: Smaug Eats Another Well-Armored and Well-Trained Adventurer Who Never Had a Smurf's Chance in a Blender." The other problem is that dragons rank second only to vampires in the list of "mythological creatures that people tend to identify a little too closely with." The level of denial is adequately illustrated by the results of the following searches on AltaVista: "I am a dragon": 157. "I am a sales clerk": 0. **C+**

Unicorns

If you weren't well acquainted with modern American culture, you might be inclined to think that unicorns were pretty cool; one-horned über-horses with a thing for virgins, chock full of psychosexual goodness. The difficulty lies not with unicorns themselves but with airbrush artists. Three decades of putting misty renditions of unicorns between the sad harlequin posters and the David Cassidy/Scott Baio/Hanson posters have made the unicorn only slightly more effective a symbol of wild purity than Pekkle the Sanrio Duck. **D**

Vampires

I could make a crack about *Vampire: The Masquerade* being Dungeons and Dragons for people who own *The Downward Spiral*, but I have a copy of all three so I'll limit myself to observing that with the increasing popularity of vampires, we're on the verge of the unicorn syndrome all over again. If it hasn't happened already, in a few months look for airbrushed posters of sad vampires in Wal-Marts everywhere, and in a decade look for female college students saying to each other, "Were you into vampires when you were nine? Me too! We were such dorks!" **C**

Mermaids

The most incredible power of mermaids, of course, is their ability to keep their hair covering their nipples at all times. Or, in the case of cartoon mermaids, the ability to wear seashell bras without bitching about the rough edges. At any rate, I don't buy the whole "sailors mistook manatees for mermaids" line. Manatees are among the least mermaidenly of all mammals. It would be easier to mistake Al Gore for a lovely young fish-woman. More likely some sailor had a thing for manatees and invented the mermaid-mistake story to keep the other sailors from ribbing him about it. **C–**

Werewolves

It's said that ancient legends have lessons for humanity, even unto the present day. The most important lesson we've learned from the legend of the werewolf is "don't cast Jack Nicholson in a role requiring him to run in slow motion." Aside from that, though, werewolves are pretty cool. You turn into a murderous, slavering wolf every full moon.

Simple yet effective, and much better than turning into a B movie–style furry guy with fangs, which to me just looks like my ninth-grade shop teacher. **B–**

Gryphons

These are the most famous example of the Grranimals school of mythical creatures, where you just take two or more sets of animal parts and jumble them together. The gryphon's combination of an eagle and a lion works pretty well. Better at least than, say, a creature with the head of a badger and the body of a potato bug. **C**

QUIZ:
ARE YOU GOD?

Yes No

☐ ☐ 1. Do you mistakenly get Buddha's mail?

☐ ☐ 2. Did you make little green apples?

☐ ☐ 3. Do your friends suddenly dump you when they start taking physics classes?

☐ ☐ 4. Do people make jokes about you liking to pretend you're a doctor?

☐ ☐ 5. Do you get pissed off when people who are not actually talking to you say your name?

☐ ☐ 6. Does your résumé consist of the single word "everything"?

☐ ☐ 7. Do you understand the success of Pauly Shore?

☐ ☐ 8. Would you, in all honesty, describe yourself as "godlike"?

☐ ☐ 9. Are people always asking you for shit?

☐ ☐ 10. Do you smite?

SCORING: Give youself one point for each "yes."

0 points:	You are not God.
1–3 points:	You are not God.
4–6 points:	You are not God.
7–9 points:	You are not God.
10 points:	You are God. Can you loan me some money?

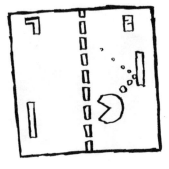

CLASSIC VIDEO GAMES

Space Invaders

There were enough "invasion from the top of the screen" games to choke a junior high school, but Space Invaders had one thing that few others did: it got faster. As you killed off the low-res interplanetary menace, the remaining would-be conquerors, fueled by revenge and freed-up CPU cycles, would steadily increase in speed, until one last Invader would be zipping across your screen like a Yorkie on crystal meth. And if you managed to shoot him down, the whole swarm would return, but closer. Yay, paranoia! **B+**

Pac-Man

The real tragedy of Pac-Man, aside from a sequel addiction that made the *Friday the Thirteenth* movies seem restrained, was that the key to the game was not skill, reflexes, or even intelligence, but rather memorization. The video games section of Waldenbooks was filled with books that told you the exact moves to make at the exact time, making mastery of Pac-Man only faintly more impressive than memorizing the first hundred digits of pi. **C–**

Night Driver

Before video game makers figured out that what you really want to do is beat up on guys with names like "Goro," they were busy turning some of the most unpleasant aspects of modern life into video games. Witness Night Driver, which was an uncanny simulation of driving a car at night when you can't see anything. Whoo! Coming soon: Night Driver II, which adds a simulation of an over-heating radiator and an eight-year-old throwing up in the backseat. **D+**

Donkey Kong

Frankly, I'm a little tired of everyone's favorite digital Italian. I think it was "Mario Teaches Typing" that did it for me. But back when Mario was a bit player and video game names were routinely poorly translated from the Japanese, there was a little story of a jumping guy, a blonde, and a giant ape with an inexplicably interminable supply of bar-rels. This was great! The music was great! The sound effects were great! That one level (out of, like, four) with the conveyor belts and the pies was great! We were pathetic then, and we didn't even care. **A–**

Tetris

If we ever meet up with an alien civilization, I'm betting they won't have Tetris, which will work to our advantage: "We have come to share the secrets of fusion, interstellar tachyon drives, and matter transfer. What do you have to offer us?"

"Um, ultimate Frisbee, microwave popcorn, and, um, Tetris."

"Hmm. Tell us of this 'Tetris.'"

"Here, give it a try."

Six months later, everyone on their planet will be staying up till four in the morning mumbling, "All I need is a straight one. Just one." And we'll have infested the cosmos like fire ants. **B**

Pong

Look. Table tennis is not that interesting of a game. TV is not that interesting of a medium. I can't imagine why combining the two was such a hit, but hey, it was the early seventies, when corduroy was king. I bought an ancient Pong game at a thrift store a while back, rushed it home, hooked it up, and within seconds I was bored. So I played "Sewer Blaster Kombat 64" instead, which was also boring, but at least it was colorful. **D+**

MORE CLASSIC VIDEO GAMES

Gauntlet

Say it with me: "Elf needs food badly. Valkyrie shot the food. Wizard is about to die." Wizard was always about to die, because Wizard was a big loser. At any rate, the designers of Gauntlet were among the first to realize that as long as you don't make them start over with every game, video game players will pump money into the machine until their joystick hands cramp up. You didn't get three lives; you got one life. And even if nothing evil touched you, said life drained away like oil from a '74 Dodge Dart. Death was inevitable, but so was hitting the change machine for another roll of quarters. **A**

Joust

Another pioneer of a video truism: It's more fun if you can "accidentally" kill a dear friend. "Oh, sorry about that, Bill. I certainly didn't mean to come barreling at you like a chicken from a jet engine testing cannon, whomping you into nothingness faster than you can say *Struthio camelus*. I was just distracted by a sudden flashback to the time when we were six and you pushed me off the swing. My bad." It's also more fun when a game has little flapping sounds, but that one hasn't endured as well. **A–**

Sinistar

Okay, maybe I'm getting a bit obscure here, but man, this was a freaky game. For those of you who got some sun in the late eighties, Sinistar was a game where you try to keep evil aliens from building a big metal face, which then hollers at you and tries to eat your spaceship. Fair enough. But what made this game stand out was the voice of the evil metal face. When it is first completed, it says, "I live!" in this deep foreboding voice that makes James Earl Jones sound like Shirley Jones by comparison. And when it roared in pain—man, first time I heard it, I leapt three feet, repented, and bit hell out of my tongue, all at once. Fun game, but tough on the nerves. **B–**

Q*bert

This just goes to show you how people can get easily impressed with new technology. This was a game so advanced, when you dropped a quarter in the slot, the machine made a noise like a quarter being dropped in the slot. An astounding display of technical wizardry! Genuine simulated quarter-dropping noises! It's almost as if you're in a real arcade, wasting actual money! It also made a mechanical thump when you dropped your little fuzzy orange guy off the edge of his video ziggurat. I assume this was an equally realistic re-creation of the noise little fuzzy guys make when impacting concrete at terminal velocity, but I've never checked. **C+**

Star Wars

This is the one where you attack a wire-frame Death Star in your wire-frame X-Wing while a presumably wire-frame dead Obi-Wan provides you with useful digitized wisdom chunks like "Let go." Letting go, obviously enough, was not a great strategy. This took a lot of liberty with the Star Wars mythos, giving us a Death Star where towers sprout up like snail eyestalks and where the trench is lined with what appear to be big tubes from a McDonald's Playland. Not to mention that there are multiple Death Stars, lined up for the plucking like grocery store cheese samples. But you know, it's fun. You shoot TIE fighters. They blow up. The Death Star explodes. Han Solo validates you. Nifty. **A**

REFERENCES FROM THAT LAST RATING

Struthio Camelus

This was completely unfair. In order to even get this, you had to know first that in Joust one of the players rides an ostrich, and secondly that *Struthio camelus* is the scientific name for a common species of ostrich. I'm sure there are about three ornithologist video game enthusiasts out there who thought this was hilarious, but really now . . . **D+**

Shirley Jones

On the other hand, I make no apologies for references to TV stars from the seventies. From Leather Tuscadero to Marshall, Will, and Holly, if they've got feathered hair and a penchant for the word "groovy," they're going to end up here sooner or later. So if you don't recognize the sacred name of the Partridge matriarch, you may want to take a remedial class or something. **A**

Ziggurat

Okay, so technically the tower in Q*bert isn't a ziggurat, partly because the little ridges don't go all around, and partly because Q*bert isn't technically Mesopotamian. But if the Mesopotamians spent less time creating the oldest legal code preserved in its entirety and more time hopping around to avoid purple snakes, I'm willing to bet the two would look eerily similar. **B–**

Jet Engine Testing Cannons

These, for those of you not "in the hip" about such things, are devices that shoot dead chickens at powered-up jet engines under controlled circumstances in order to determine whether said engines can survive the impact, the chicken's survival being a moot point. There's a story about someone inadvertently using frozen chickens that's too unlikely to reprint here, but it serves to illustrate that there's actually already a distinguished body of dead chicken cannon literature out there, of which this space is only a small part. **C+**

'74 Dodge Dart

This may shock some of the faithful, but I actually have no idea how prone to oil leaks Dodge Darts are. I had a friend who had a lot of trouble with hers, though, and "Dodge Dart" is a funny name (and good advice, when you think about it), so rather than spend time going through maintenance history for hundreds of American cars, I just went with it. I'd like to say I used the time saved to create new and better comedy for your consumption, but actually I made a grilled cheese sandwich and took a "test your kiss-ability" quiz in *YM*. **C**

SUPER FRIENDS

Aquaman

Let's face it, Aquaman basically got suck for powers. His major shtick was the whole concentric-ring-exuding fish-control thing that allowed him to draft underwater life-forms into his own personal war, which of course required the writers of the show to work a major marine disaster into every ensemble piece. This demonstrates a central flaw in including Aquaman on the team: having water-based powers is a pretty serious limitation, along the lines of having superpowers that only work on weekends. **C–**

Batman

Batman gets extra points for having the best line in the entire history of the Super Friends. The villain was named Dr. Noah Tall or something equally ludicrous, and he and his evil little sidekick were posed as street-corner food vendors with a cart and everything. As part of their plan, they were attempting to get Batman to buy some chicken soup. This *really happened, dammit!* Anyhow, Batman, the dark night detective, the scourge of the underworld, assessing the situation with his keen crime-fighting brain, asks, in his deep, stentorian voice, "Is the chicken soup fresh?" It was a glorious moment. **A**

Superman

Oh, what are you going to say about Superman? He's got it all going on. It's really good that he's such a nice guy, because if I were in Superman's place, I'd be totally lording my powers over all the other Super Friends. "Hey, Batman," I'd say, "nice utility belt! Got anything in there that would help you lift an oil tanker? I didn't think so. Hey, Aquaman! You realize I could pretty much kick ass over any sea creature you cared to summon, don't you? Wonder Woman! Your magic lasso makes me tell the truth: You suck!" So I suppose we should be grateful. **B–**

Wonder Woman

Wonder Woman has a grab bag of powers and equipment, as if she had picked everything up from the superhero equivalent of the Sharper Image catalog. She had the Bullet-Reflecting Bracelets ($29.95), the Mind-Control Lasso ($38.95) and of course the Invisible Plane ($150,000 plus taxes and license fees). That last one always got to me. It's like a regular plane, only it's invisible. It doesn't make *her* invisible, though. So instead of this big plane, you see a nice inconspicuous flying squatting woman. Huh. **B–**

Wendy and Marvin and Wonder Dog

What? What? Why are these losers hanging out with the Super Friends? Did they win some sort of lame-ass contest? Are they somebody's cousins? Wendy didn't even *try* to fit in with the superhero crowd, and the best Marvin could do was a towel around his neck and a T-shirt that said "M." And then there was the dog. There's something really sad in the fact that the Super Friends were hanging out with Scooby-Doo wannabes for so long. **D**

Zan and Jayna

I don't know if it was every fully explained why Wendy and Marvin were replaced by Donny and Marie Osmond in

Spock ears, but then Wendy and Marvin's presence was never adequately explained in the first place. Zan and Jayna were a definite improvement, because not only were neither of them named Marvin, they also had cool powers. Zan's ability to turn into water objects would have been a bit lame if not for the ice sculpture loophole, but Jayna definitely was happening with her animal transformation. Could have done without that Gleek organism, though. **C+**

MORE SUPER FRIENDS

Green Lantern

At first glance, GL seems like the only Super Friend who's up to Superman levels of power. He can make anything he wants just by thinking about it, plus he has a snazzy outfit. But then there's his weakness: yellow. A primary color, for God's sake! "Big Bird! You have defeated me once again!" "Lemon-scented dishwashing liquid! Lo! I am foiled!" "Marshmallow peeps! Nooooooo!" Nice try. But it's a very snazzy outfit. **C+**

Apache Chief

A typical seventies cultural compromise: "We'll include multicultural heroes in our cartoon series, but we're going to give them lame powers. No, I mean really lame." Thus, we have Apache Chief ("Oh, and we're going to give them stupid names, too"), who can grow big. And once he turned into a bear. That's fine for "Tall Tales of the Pioneers," but one would hope for something a little more riveting from the spandex-and-superpower crowd. His saving grace was that he had a great magic word, which various Internet sources list as "Inec CHOCH," "Enek-CHUK," or "Noam CHOMSKY." **C**

Hawkman

Hawkman has a good name and a good look, but when the Legion of Doom hits town, you have to admit that he's just basically a guy with wings, and that doesn't inspire a lot of confidence. Half the Super Friends can fly already, all of them can do something else besides, and none of them molt. **C–**

The Flash

I like the Flash. Granted, Superman has the speed thing down, too, but it's always nice to have a backup speedster. That's really the problem with expanding the Super Friends; you really start to double up on the superpower niches. Then you get eight different people trying to capture the same bad guy, mitigate the same natural disaster, or convince the same preteen not to chew on Styrofoam cup edges, and the natural jealousy and resentment that follows leads to tension and the inevitable front-page breakup, with several of the team members trying to re-form under the name "The Friends," which in turn leads to a long, drawn-out trademark infringement suit, alienating the core fan base, who turn to marijuana and imported porn comics as a means of dealing with the crushing disappointment of seeing their idols revealed as flawed human beings like anyone else, and meanwhile Gorilla Grodd is dancing on the mayor's head and nobody's doing anything about it. So you see. **C+**

Black Vulcan

Another from the Great Melting Pot of Lame Powers, Black Vulcan's power was "whatever we feel like, as long as we make it look electric-like." For instance, to fly, he turned his lower body into lightning. I don't see how that would propel you, seeing as your lower body would then be attracted to the ground or any large grounded metal objects, but if we start questioning the physics of the Super Friends, we're going to have to start with "Isn't Robin chilly in that getup?" And that would take up a four-unit elective class by itself. **C**

Firestorm

Technically, Firestorm didn't show up until *Super Friends* had become *Super Friends: The Legendary Super Powers Show*, but his head's on fire, so that makes up for it. Firestorm could transform substances into other substances, as long as they weren't organic, so again we're dealing with someone who has no power to affect many common household objects such as yams and leather checkbook covers. It would have been much more entertaining if his weakness was limited to organic produce, because then we could have had episodes with titles like "Showdown at the Farmer's Market" and "The Legumes of Doom." **C+**

CRYPTOZOOLOGICAL CREATURES

Bigfoot

Also called Sasquatch by people who feel that a less goofy name will lend blurry pictures of swaggering hominids more authority. I doubt this tactic works. Nobody doubts the existence of the blue-footed booby, do they? Plus, "bigfoot" makes a much better name for pizza, beer, and monster trucks. **B**

Loch Ness Monster

The problem with lake monsters is that they don't have the danger factor. If they exist, apparently they're large, water bound, and slow moving. Proving they exist would be like proving your brother-in-law has been sleeping on your couch. Sure, it's good to know, but it lacks drama. If pictures of plesiosaurs wearing tam-o'-shanters weren't so goshdamn compelling, I'm sure the Loch Ness monster wouldn't get so much press. **D+**

Yeti

Some people seem to lump yeti—along with skunk apes, yowies, and yerens—in with bigfoots. I find it funny that we don't know that these beasties even exist and people are already making up family trees for them. It's like creating an evolutionary tree showing that Keebler elves and Santa's elves evolved from a common ancestor. **C–**

Chupacabras

I like any creature that gives me the excuse to use the word "exsanguination." The Chupacabra's talents aren't limited to the exsanguination (yeah!) of farm animals, though. Jesus, no! According to *ParaScope* magazine, Joe Espinoza of Tucson, Arizona, claims that a Chupacabra entered his home and "briefly sat atop Espinoza's seven-year-old son." An animal that both sucks the blood out of goats *and* sits on grade-schoolers begs one question: Why hasn't this thing been domesticated yet? They sound much more fun than potbellied pigs, which were popular about the same time and for about as long as Chupacabras were. Coincidence? Yes! **B**

Mokele-mbembe

The Mokele-mbembe (pronounced to rhyme with "Fokele-fbembe") is allegedly a brontosaurus-like creature that lives in the Congo. Depending on what poorly formatted Web page you look at, the name means "one who stops the flow of rivers," "one who eats the tops of palm trees," or "half god, half beast." All of which sound like boastful penis nicknames. They even made a movie about this guy. You know, if Hollywood is telling the truth—and it is—all we need to do to find any given mystery animal is to send an evil scientist after it. A team of good scientists will immediately go in to save it, and they will eventually succeed and probably fall in love in the process. **A**

QUIZ:
IS THAT HAM?

1. What's in these little egg things? It tastes like ham.
   - ☐ It's ham.
   - ☐ It's not ham.
2. Look. There's little pink bits. They look like ham.
   - ☐ They're ham.
   - ☐ Those are not ham.
3. Smell that. Smell it! Tell me that's not ham.
   - ☐ Okay, it's ham.
   - ☐ I'm telling you, it's not ham.
4. The hamlike bits are sort of chewy.
   I'm pretty sure they're ham.
   - ☐ Yeah, that *is* ham.
   - ☐ That's not ham.
5. No, really. It's ham. What else could it be?
   It's got to be ham.
   - ☐ It's ham.
   - ☐ It's not ham.

SCORING: Give yourself one point for each pro-ham answer.

0 points:	That is so not ham.
1–2 points:	It's probably not ham. I don't know what it is, though. Something hamlike.
3–5 points:	I think it's ham. It's probably ham. Let's just say it's ham.
6 points:	Yep, that's ham, all right.

RULES FOR MY
APARTMENT COMPLEX

Cars May Not Be Painted in Psychedelic Colors

This, I have to say, was a huge disappointment, given that I traditionally celebrate moving into each new apartment with a reenactment of the "Can You Picture That" number from *The Muppet Movie*, using my 1997 Toyota Corolla in lieu of a Studebaker. Thwarted in this, I am forced instead to stand atop it and sing "Never Before" in a Miss Piggy voice, and I don't see how that's going to make my neighbors any happier. **C–**

No Drinking in the Common Area

Looking around the apartment complex, I can only assume that I got a bad copy of the rental agreement and that the actual rule is "No drinking in the common area unless you have your shirt off." Or possibly, "No drinking in the common area, except for watery American beer, which frankly is so low in alcohol it can practically drive in some states." **C**

No Bottle or Cans in the Window

The rules thus far, taken as a whole, remind me of a high-strung upper-class woman desperately trying to cover up for her husband's alcoholism. "For God's sake, Henry, it's bad enough that you've turned yourself into a pathetic mockery of adulthood, but do you have to ruin my life, too? I'm not asking that much, dammit! Just keep your drinking inside, your stinking cans and bottle off the windowsill, and for Christ's sake, don't go on one of your benders and paint the car fluorescent pink again! Just do that for me and you can drink yourself to death for all I care!" **C–**

No Slamming of Refrigerator Doors

This comes well within the category of "things I had no interest in doing until they were forbidden to me." I've never been mad enough at the contents of my fridge to slam the door, although I once had some liverwurst that pissed me off pretty bad. And refrigerators have that puffy lining around the door that keeps them from slamming effectively, anyway. But now that I've been expressly told not to slam it, I feel put out and ready to take this one to the Supreme Court. **D**

No Snorkels in the Pool

I'm really perplexed by this one. Do they consider snorkels unsightly? Dangerous? Perverse? Does the property owner just refuse to believe that the word "snorkel" really exists? I suppose it could be to prevent people from slipping on snorkels left by the side of the pool and cracking their fool heads open, but there's no rule against, say, toy fire trucks. Weird. **D+**

Apartment Must Be Used Solely as a Dwelling Unit

I assume that by this they mean that it must be used only as a home and not as, say, the headquarters and production center for a Web-based comedy magazine. Once again I find myself living in the shadowy boundaries of a rental agreement, where right and wrong give way to questions of whether I'll get my deposit back. It's a hard life, but it's the life I've chosen. **D–**

SCOOBY-DOO CHARACTERS

Scooby-Doo

Is it just me, or is there something eerie about Scooby? He's not anthropomorphic, exactly, he just speaks English. With a canine accent. As if trying to force his tortured vocal cords to form sounds that no loving god ever intended. Was he the result of some madman's blasphemous experiments in creating life? Are the ghosts he's chasing really the ghosts of his own inhuman mind? Should I get out more? **B**

Scrappy-Doo

Speaking of inhuman. I just want to get this twisted little bastard out of the way so that I can go back to ignoring him. The more astute readers among you may have noticed that I haven't yet gone so far as to give anything an actual "F." That's not out of any kindheartedness on my part; it's just that every time I got ready to give one out, I would ask myself, "Is it really that bad, compared to the verminous, soul-tainting badness of Scrappy-Doo?" And now, at long last, I have my chance. Prepare yourself, oh encephalitic hound. **F!** Hahahahahaha! It feels good!

Fred

Man. Post-catharsis, I'm feeling pretty charitable toward the entire rest of the animated gang. Heck, I could probably give Quick Draw McGraw a passing grade at this point. However, objectivity is in order. Fred's dull. He's one bland blond. He's a six-foot yawn in a cravat. His big thought every episode is "let's split up," and he apparently takes fashion tips from Mr. Howell. **C–**

Shaggy

Hey, I'm way behind anyone voiced by Casey Kasem. Shaggy, Robin, Cliffjumper from *The Transformers*, anyone. I bet Casey and Don Pardo get together and go to bars and enunciate clearly. But I digress. Shaggy. Blah blah pot blah blah hippie blah blah munchies. Every half-assed stand-up comedian from here to the Catskills has a bit on the Shaggy-reefer connection. But they don't understand about Casey. Casey's the alpha and the omega of Hanna-Barbera. That's all there is to say. **A–**

Velma

This one wins the prestigious "Cartoon Character Whose Name I Have to Look Up Most Often" award. Velma? Thelma? Selma, Alabama? Anyhow, while Fred's getting fashion advice from Thurston, Velma apparently gets her look from a beanbag that went to Catholic school. She does seem to have more wits about her than the rest of her gang, but saying she's the brains of the group is like saying someone has the best social skills of anyone on Ultima Online. **B–**

Daphne

I guess she's supposed to be the beauty of the group, but nobody looks that great at eight frames per second. Whereas Fred was merely dull, Daphne was dull and pointless. Fred at least bossed people around. Aside from chastising Shaggy and Scooby and getting caught in the inevitable net trap, Daphne didn't really have much to do. So of course she's the one they hang on to for the pathetic *13 Ghosts of Scooby-Doo* series. Pleh. **D**

MONOPOLY TOKENS

The Doggie

Ah, yes. The Gleaming Terrier of Finance. As a kid, the selling point of the dog was that you could tilt him and pretend to make him piddle on your opponents' hotels. Not exactly evolved comedy, but once you've chuckled over the "Beauty Contest" card, you have to take your laughs where you can get them in Monopoly. **C**

The Shoe

Okay, fine, shoe equals walk equals travel around the board. But what I want to know is, what the hell is that on the back of the shoe? I mean, in practical terms it's a handle, but the car doesn't have a random protrusion coming out of the back, so why does the shoe? Is it a shoehorn? Was there a penchant for wearing strap-enhanced footwear during the Great Depression? Weird. Eerie. **C–**

The Car

Now this is the piece to have. The movement metaphor is there, as is the reference to riches. The sound effects were de rigueur, of course, with the car screeching through the visiting area of the jail like a Duke boy. Nice set of wheels, too. I wonder if there's someplace you can buy a replica Monopoly car. That'd turn heads at the classic auto show. **A**

The Hat

Yawn. "Hey, I'm a hat. Here I am. A hat. Felt, you know. Bask in my haberdashery." I'm sorry, maybe I wasn't paying attention in freshman drama class, but I just can't get into the role of a hat that invests in real estate. It sounds like a bad remake of an old live-action Disney movie. **D**

The Guy on a Horse

What game is this token really from? What is it doing in Monopoly? It's fun and all, if a tad unstable and prone to getting stepped on and bent, but how does "ride 'em, cowboy" fit in with "fork over the rent, you peon"? Maybe it's a reference to polo or something, but it sure looks like the Hopalong Cassidy school of equestrianism to me. **B**

The One Everyone Forgets

What was it? I keep thinking "candlestick," but that's Clue. Martini glass? Wad of bills? Bishop? I'm pretty sure I've seen a silver battleship, but either that's just that expanded edition they were hawking a while ago, or I'm getting mental board game cross-pollination again. Well, it couldn't have been all that great, so I'll give it the generic stamp of mild disapproval. **C–**

GOOD LUCK CHARMS

Horseshoe

Sure, why not. There's probably some goddess-crescent connection here, and if there isn't, I'm sure there are plenty of liberal arts undergrads willing to make one up. My favorite part is how you're supposed to keep your lucky horseshoe's ends up "to keep the luck from pouring out." Because you don't want to have a doorstep covered in luck, which will enter the sewage system during the next rain and drain to the ocean, resulting in unnaturally fortunate salmon. The resulting devastating impact on the ecosystem is easy to envision. So watch it. **B**

Rabbit's Foot

Yeah, yeah, it wasn't lucky for the rabbit, we've all heard that one about a million times, and the only reason I even mention it is to avoid mail "reminding" me of this "oversight." Even so, I find rabbit's feet a little gruesome to pin my personal fortunes to. I don't want to be put in the position of saying "I owe all my success and acclaim to this dismembered mammal limb I keep with me." **D**

Shooting Star

That's right, an isolated chunk of interstellar grit traversed uncounted miles of cold space, then fell into the sea of our atmosphere and died in a slashing trail of flame so that you could wish for a new set of speakers for your Chevy Tahoe. I mean, astrology also assumes heavenly objects determine whether it's a good time to buy a new shirt, but at least astrology doesn't require Venus to crash into the earth to do so. On the other hand, shooting stars are pretty. **A–**

Lucky Penny

"Find a penny, pick it up, and all the day you'll have good luck." Does this apply to convenience-store penny trays? You possess the penny for an instant before handing it to the clerk, don't you? You found it, you picked it up. My God, this could revolutionize the science of random prosperity. It could take its place among other examples of modern luck-generation innovations such as the steam-powered wishing well and Rainbow Brite. **C+**

Four-Leaf Clover

I imagine most good luck charms have an annoying song associated with them if you look hard enough (e.g., "Lucky Star") but this one is just out of control. I don't know if it was the traditional "Sing Along with Mitch" version or the gory schoolyard parody that made it impossible for me to consider clover of any variety—even clover honey—without hearing ". . . that I overlooked be*fore!*" echoing insanely through my head, but I don't like it. **C–**

COCA-COLA SLOGANS

"Drink Coca-Cola" (1886)

This was the original slogan. I understand advertising was much less reliant on mountain bikes and navel-baring tube tops in the 1800s than it is now. This is the quintessential Coca-Cola slogan; it's short, it's vaguely authoritarian, and it completely fails to actually give any reasons why you should drink Coke. This is because you can't actually convince anyone they need Coke. You either like the taste or you don't, and it doesn't provide you with any benefits you can't get from other places, such as hummingbird feeders. Their ad campaigns are instead based on making sure that everyone who would ever consider drinking Coke never forgets for an instant that the option is available. Anyhow, this at least is simple and to the point. **A–**

"I'd Like to Buy the World a Coke" (1971)

This was an offshoot of the unfortunate ad jingle turned folk song I was forced to sing too many times in grade school. The song was, among other things, about teaching the world to sing in perfect harmony, which is pretty ironic because most of the people I've heard sing it were in no position to be giving lessons. Don't get me wrong, I'm all in favor of starry-eyed idealism, but not when it's being used to sell soda pop, and especially not when it contains forced lines about snow-white turtledoves. **D**

"Coke Adds Life" (1976)

They missed out on a great chance for an ad here. Scene: the Garden of Eden, circa 4004 B.C. God (looking not unlike the Coke-swilling Santa Claus of yore) forms Adam from the dust, humming mildly to himself as he does so. When Adam's prone and lifeless form is complete, God dribbles a couple drops of Coca-Cola onto his lips. Adam blinks, sits up, and sees the Big Guy holding an icy-cold bottle of Coke. Being only recently made of dust, he's parched, and he reaches out to God in a pose strongly reminiscent of the Sistine Chapel. "Coca-Cola Adds Life." Boom, instant megahit. They could have followed up with a series of Old Testament Coke ads, and eventually released the Bible, Revised Caffeinated Edition. **C+**

"Coke Is It" (1982)

At this point they've gone from authoritarian to positively Orwellian. "Coke Is All There Is," the slogan seems to imply. "All Is Coke. There Are No Other Forms of Refreshment. Drink Coke or Die Screaming." Armed, jack-booted Cola Enforcers roam the streets, dragging off anyone caught with a can of Mountain Dew. Children in school pledge allegiance to Coke. History books mentioning Pepsi are burned in secret. Red flags with jaunty white ribbons running across them snap sternly in the hot wind. "Coke. Do Not Attempt to Escape." **A**

"Red, White, and You" (1986)

This was a result of the doomed New Coke fiasco. The Coca-Cola company, whipped into shame by people who never protested when their ketchup or paper towels were "improved," rereleases Coca-Cola Classic with this lame slogan. The ominous pronouncements of past campaigns are replaced with a wheedling humanist attempt to get people to identify themselves with Coca-Cola. Before, Coke was above mere humans; it was a force of history, a societal universal. Now it's a touchy-feely hands-on Soft Drink of the People. "Coke Feels Your Pain." **D–**

"Always Coca-Cola" (1993)

Now we're getting back into the familiar realms of over-statement. Coke already trades on nostalgia to an alarming extent, especially come Christmastide. This slogan, I think, is an attempt to pioneer the powerful advertising concept of "pre-nostalgia." Teen cola drinkers are too young to have misty memories of days gone by, but Coca-Cola assures them that one day they'll miss their days of looking forward to the time when they can look back fondly on their youthful exuberance for their nostalgic future. And Coca-Cola will have been there. **B**

SESAME STREET CHARACTERS

Cookie Monster

Cookie is the *man!* Cookie's got it *all* going on! Cookie is a huge terry cloth mass of greed, gluttony, and astonishing lack of self-restraint, and this is on *educational TV!* And Cookie Monster, in his Zenlike wisdom, provided my generation with perhaps the only clear moral message we'll ever know, a beacon for our scattered lives: "C is for cookie, and that's good enough for me." It's good enough for all of us, Cookie. **A**

Elmo

I know lots of people are enamored of this Muppet-come-lately, and I have to admit I have no idea why. Elmo is this completely harmless, sweet, friendly toddler-monster, and he bores the hell out of me. He lacks the joie de vivre of his predecessors; you'd never see Elmo tearing apart huge Styrofoam vowels, yelling angrily at passersby, or even "doing the pigeon." Instead of bizarre antisocial behavior and physical comedy, we get cute childlike antics and "tickling." Pleh. **D–**

Oscar the Grouch

Mean people may suck, but Oscar rocks. I always enjoyed Oscar's bit where he's happy when he's angry and angry when he's happy, but I never knew I'd be emulating him someday. Oscar is another example of a character that wouldn't even be considered if Sesame Street were being created today. Instead they'd slip some Zoloft in his feed, transplant him to a brightly colored recycled oil drum, and have him lead "Ring Around the Rosie." **A–**

Bert and Ernie

Yeah, yeah. Were they just roommates or were they lovers? Listen, folks, they were Muppets. They may have had hands up their asses, but it was purely for puppeteering purposes. Besides, for my money, the real sexual tension was between Grover and Kermit. Anyhow, Ernie and Bert always had the song-and-dance thing down pat. Ernie's "Rubber Ducky" song is the Sesame Street classic, and Bert's "Doing the Pigeon" had similar appeal, plus a really unnerving dance move. And then there was the bit where their noses got pulled off. Always fun. **B**

The Count

Man, talk about a twisted personality! Talk about obsessive-compulsive disorder! Talk about the numbers one through twelve! You really couldn't get the Count into any long-term plots because he really only did one thing, but he certainly did it well. I think many children learned to count purely on the off chance that they could summon thunder and lightning by doing so. But I have one question. The Count looked like a vampire, right down to the fangs. And he had the bat thing going. Was he a vampire? Did he feed on living blood? Or, more likely given his Muppetness, living felt? A horrifying yet oddly appealing idea. **B–**

Big Bird

The name was kind of a gimme. Big Bird is somewhat less twisted than most of the Muppets around him, but due to his intimidating size and lack of baby lisp, he doesn't have the repulsive Elmo cuteness. In the early days he had a kind of lovable loser image going, with all his hallucinations, and his calling Mr. Hooper "Mr. Looper," but Hooper/Looper took the dirt nap and Snuffy showed himself to everyone, so BB's in a much more capable place now. **C+**

FLOWERS

Roses

It would be difficult to come up with a better symbol for romantic love than the rose. Because it is beautiful and smells lovely, yes, and because the petals feel like soft skin, but mostly because they hurt like hell if you're not careful. This is why I am completely opposed to thornless roses. Roses without thorns are the floral equivalent of the word "luv." **A**

Lilies

Lilies are lovely, no doubt, especially calla lilies of funereal fame, but I think the big warty orange pistils don't help. They put me in the mind of tall, somber mourners with heads bowed, but more precisely tall, somber mourners who just drank orange Kool-Aid, going "bleeeeaaaah." **C+**

Carnations

The first problem with carnations is that they don't have a scent. They really seem like they ought to, but smelling one is like trying to turn on one of those hollow plastic fake TVs they have at furniture stores. They're also a really popular flower in low-end floral arrangements at supermarkets, so in my mind they say, "You mean $2.39 to me." But they do look good in the lapels of well-attired tap dancers and mob enforcers alike. **C–**

Baby's Breath

What a weird name. I can't say whether there's supposed to be an olfactory correlation here, because I haven't checked any babies for surreptitious drinking lately, but I wouldn't be surprised if it were originally called "toad weed" or something and an enterprising florist came up with this alternative. **D+**

Daisies

I think the main reason daisies loom so large in the pantheon of posies is that they're the easiest flower to draw. Comic strips are full of shy or repentant paramours handing over a bunch of symmetrical daisies, all of which just happen to be facing the viewer. Think about it, when's the last time you saw a drawing of the back of a daisy? **C–**

Poppies

Poppies will always be known as much for their association with drugs as for their inherent attractiveness, just like black light posters and Drew Barrymore. I always assumed that opium poppies were some sort of exotic breed that was only grown in areas without regular helicopter traffic, but no, you can order them from seed catalogs. I'm not clear on when it becomes illegal to grow them, but I imagine it hinges on your ability to say "Why, officer, I had no idea these were *that* sort of poppy" with a straight face. **B**

QUIZ:
ARE YOU DEAD?

Yes No

☐ ☐ 1. Are you dressed in the nicest outfit you own?

☐ ☐ 2. Has your life insurance company stopped sending you bills?

☐ ☐ 3. Try being right about something. Were you dead right?

☐ ☐ 4. When your local bar has "People Who Aren't Dead Night," do you still have to pay a cover charge?

☐ ☐ 5. Do you feel an unexplainable affinity with doornails?

☐ ☐ 6. Are you getting a lot of junk mail from crematories?

☐ ☐ 7. Have you canceled your subscriptions to *Life* and *Martha Stewart Living?*

☐ ☐ 8. Have you experienced that uncomfortable feeling you get when you're talking to a guy and you realize he has your corneas?

☐ ☐ 9. Are necrophiliacs always coming on to you?

☐ ☐ 10. Do you no longer have the song "Love Shack" stuck in your head?

Multiply your number of "yes" answers by ten to get your percentage of deadness:

0% Dead:

You're alive! You live and breathe and feel and experience! But you'll be dead eventually anyway.

10%–90% Dead:

You're still alive, and more so than Boris Yeltsin, at least.

100% Dead:

Time to close the book and rest in peace. You've earned it.

ASPECTS OF
THE PERSONALS

Friendship

Is there anyone, even one person, who honestly shells out cash to a newspaper to look for friendship and nothing more? I'm not talking about "book club forming"–style ads, I mean the ones that sound just like the usual "soul mate/pillow bunny wanted" ads, except that they end "let's be friends." I don't know what's sadder, the idea that these people have found normal outlets for friendship such as the Kiwanis Club or protest marches unfruitful, or the idea that they're lying, throbbing-crotch bastards who don't want to be friends any more than a used car dealer wants to give you the best deal in town. **C–**

Long Walks on the Beach

My local independent weekly, the *Independent Weekly*, lists fifteen people who like walks, eighteen who like the beach, two who like walks on the beach, three who like long walks, and one who likes long walks on the beach. Those of you who find cliché to be irresistible have a lot to choose from. **D**

Euphemisms for "Not Fat"

The most common here is "slim," but some people seem to be very shy about coming out and saying that they consider Nancy Reagan to have an ideal body type. This leads to such odd circumlocutions as "height/weight proportional" (proportional to whom? Michael Stipe? Michael Moore?), "fit" (which could conceivably include wide-hipped bicyclists but which I've always taken to be short for "able to fit into a size two"), and "sleek" ("a woman, she should be like the ferret"). You're not fooling anybody, you *Maxim*-soiling frat ape, so come out and say it. **D**

Therapy Terms

Were I looking to meet a paramour and/or party girl through the personals, the one thing guaranteed to give me the wriggling squirms would be those ads that sound as if they were literal transcriptions of a therapist's advice: "I'm leaving my baggage behind. Can you leave yours? SWF seeks SWM with listening skills and no abandonment issues for validation, support, hot zebu sex." No amount of hot zebu sex is worth that. **D+**

Missed Connections

These things always sound as if they were written by people who would be stalkers if they had more time off. A typical template would be "I saw you at a public place, where you were wearing nondescript clothing. You acknowledged my existence in a noncommittal manner. I regret not acting like a creepy dork then, would like a second chance." **C–**

ASPECTS OF BOWLING

Air Blower Things

These are those little vents on the bowling ball receiving unit where you put your fingers to dry off the sweat that accumulates from the sheer tension of playing such a challenging game in borrowed shoes. For me, these are one of the main pleasures of the game. I like to pretend I went to get a manicure between frames and I'm drying my nails. In fact, I'm so into this part of bowling that I can't use those hand dryers they have in cheapskate public rest rooms, because it gives me this incredible urge to go bowling, which frightens and alienates my friends. **B+**

Beer

Beer is one of the main selling points of bowling. Bowling, along with softball and darts, is one of the premier beer sports. It sounds fun, but there's a catch: The beer served at bowling alleys is swill. It's possible that the watery nature of bowling alley beer is due to safety concerns, to keep patrons from getting wasted and loosing sixteen-pound, four-hole bowling balls at one another's heads, but more likely it's just part of the greater rule that you can't get decent beer anyplace where you find a lot of people with their names on their shirts. **D+**

Brunswick

For years I referred to that big plank that came down and swept away the seven or so pins I inevitably left standing as a "Brunswick." Because, after all, that's what was written across the front of it. Eventually it dawned on me that everything in a bowling alley has "Brunswick" written on it: balls, ball return units, exceptionally devoted employees, and so on. The Brunswick Corporation apparently has some sort of lock on the bowling industry. That's okay, though, because "Brunswick" is one of the coolest words in the English language or something very like it. I wish it were a swear word so that I'd have more opportunity to use it. "Get your Brunswick the Brunswick out of there, you Brunswick!" **A–**

Communal Bowling Balls

The problem with professional bowling, of course, is that the scores are too high. A strike is quite an epiphany for me when I make my first one in six or seven games, but the empathetic thrill of watching some guy on TV make a strike wears off after eight or nine in a row. My solution is to make the professionals use randomly selected communal alley balls. These things are great. Not only do the lighter ones come in all sorts of gaudy Eva Gabor hues, but each and every one of them appears to have been questioned under torture. I bowled one of my best games with a ball that seemed to have a large bite taken out of it, with actual teeth marks and everything. **A**

Shoes

I don't buy this whole disinfectant scam. These shoes have been worn by hundreds of people, from all sorts of cretinous walks of life, and they figure a little spritz of whatever's in those cans is going to restore them to springtime sanitary freshness. Uh-huh. That's like spending three weeks sacking out in a public rest room, then being offered a Tic Tac. Of course there's the old "let's make them ugly so no one steals them" scheme. Aside from the fact that in today's youth-oriented fashion world, butt-ugly shoes are a major coup, do they really think that anyone who's going to make off with battered communal shoes is worried about whether they go with his Dockers? **C–**

Actual Bowling

It's okay. **C**

STAR WARS VILLAINS

Darth Vader

There's nothing to say. Darth is it. He's the eight-hundred-pound gorilla of the Force, Mr. Light Saber himself, the Dark Lord of the Sith. He's got the admiral-choking power, the kick-ass mask, the intimidating rasp, the jet-black TIE fighter, and the James Earl Jones voice-overs. I don't care what Obi-Wan says, this is a man who made some good career choices. **A+**

Grand Moff Tarkin

It's hard to take a villain seriously when he has "Moff" in his title. Tarkin was nasty enough with his deeply etched scowl and his Aryan stride, and obviously he had enough going for him that Vader didn't give him the old long-distance esophagus hand job, but when the chips were down and Red Five was going in, he made the Bad Choice. Vader cleverly managed to survive the destruction of the Death Star and still come out looking like a total stud, but El Moff Grande just ended up as the third cinder from the left in the upper right-hand corner of your screen. **C**

Stormtroopers

"Only Imperial Stormtroopers are so precise," said Obi-Wan in one of his less stunningly accurate pronouncements.

Obi must have gotten a little too much sun during his Tattooine holiday, because as the rest of the movie shows, Imperial Stormtroopers couldn't hit the sidewalk with a can of paint. If that's not bad enough, they're also easily intimidated and dumber than monkey chow. Still, they've got nifty uniforms and there's buttloads of them, so they make excellent fodder for the good guys. **B–**

Boba Fett

Another from the mask-and-armor school of villainy, Boba Fett had a lot going for him. Not only did he pack lots of cool gadgets such as grappling hooks and a jet pack, he also had the wherewithal to track down Han Solo. Fett was the only one who didn't fall for the old "drift away with their garbage" trick, and thanks to that, he was the one to deliver the Hansicle to Jabba and stick around for the party. Unfortunately, now he's doing the new definition of pain and suffering thing in the Sarlacc Pit. **B**

Jabba the Hutt

"Hutt" is right up there with "Moff" in the list of "words it's best not to have in your name if you want to be intimidating." Jabba actually lacks a lot of qualities necessary to be a really first-rate bad guy. Mobility is one of them. Lack of resemblance to escargot is another. He's got some mean pets and interesting ideas for torture, but he's really too party-oriented to make it as a villain. I mean, could you take out Vader using only a length of chain while wearing a metal bikini? I think not. **C**

Sandpeople

I was never able to figure out whether "Tusken Raiders" referred to the fact that they had little tusklike thingies on their masks, or that they were from a town called Tusken, or what. They were mean, though, with the scary faces and the rags for clothes and the Gaffi Sticks with the spikes on the end and the big furry elephants to stomp the unassuming homes of hapless moisture farmers. But then, all you have to do is learn to make that noise that Ben Kenobi made and they're off like rabbits, even in mid-clobber, which kind of cuts down on their effectiveness. **C+**

FISHER-PRICE LITTLE PEOPLE

Lucky the Dog

Lucky has reason to be happy, in spite of the fashion faux pas of a spiked collar in fire-engine red. Being of similar dimensions as the rest of the family, he has attained equal status. He fits on the merry-go-round! He can sit behind the desk! He can drive the ambulance! If the real world were more like the Fisher-Price world, we'd have happier dogs and more people bleeding to death on the freeway asphalt. **B+**

The Father

I'm guessing on the relationships among the Little People, here. It's not like you can check for a wedding ring. At any rate, the Standard Fisher-Price Little Adult Male Person apparently went to Charlie Brown Beauty College for all his haircuts. But he seems to be happy with his lot; wife, children, plastic car with circular depressions for seats. It's all a Fisher-Price Person could ask for. **C**

The Upset Freckled Boy Child

It's nice of Fisher-Price to include a dissident among all the smiling Little Constantly Happy People. A dissident with his hat on sideways, so you know he's trouble. He's unquestionably the sort of hard-hearted delinquent who steals apples from Old Man Croody's yard and says "Nuts to you!" to authority figures. I like him. **A**

The Mother

Mom's freaky. Her eyes are always closed, and her mouth is always open, like some sort of deformed baby bird. Maybe the open mouth is supposed to be a smile, but in that case she has pink teeth, which is its own set of problems. Combine that with a stern German headmistress hairdo, and you've got one unnerving hausfrau. Also, she has no nose. **D+**

The Little Girl

Continuing with the Aryan theme of the distaff portion of the Little People world, the little girl seems to be going for a "Heidi of the Nontoxic Plastic Alps" look, what with her milkmaid braids and the cute little ruff between her head and thorax. No doubt once she reaches puberty her nose will fall off and her eyes will glue shut and she'll end up just like dear old Mom. She may build a cocoon first, I'm not sure. **C–**

CLUE SUSPECTS

Disclaimer: This is not based on the movie. The movie is of no consequence. This Ratings goes directly to the cardboard-encased source: the Parker Brothers game.

Colonel Mustard

A man among men. A hearty adventurer who grabs life with both hands and stuffs it into his mouth like so much canned chili, making chorfing sounds all the while. A ladies' man, a gentleman's gentleman, and a closet cross-dresser, Colonel Mustard, bastard half-brother of the Beatles' Mean Mr. Mustard, could probably kill Mr. Boddy, grind him up and serve him to the jurors in their city-hall-cafeteria enchiladas, and still get off scot-free. **A**

Mrs. Peacock

Peacock is a color? And it's light blue? I've seen peacocks—abrasive, parasite-ridden birds with a cry like a drowning drunk crow—and as far as I've been able to tell, light blue is not part of their admittedly impressive display. It's hard for me to imagine that a Valium-addled society matron like Mrs. Peacock would be able to crack someone's skull with a single deft blow of an eight-pound candlestick, but if there's a way we can frame actual peacocks for this crime, I'm all for it. **C+**

Miss Scarlet

A cunning seductress with a smile like the clink of a poisoned wine glass and a heart of cold, hard cash. Even if Miss Scarlet didn't do it, she probably would have gotten around to it sooner or later; if there's one thing made clear from the game, it's that Boddy was loaded, and what Scarlet wants, Scarlet gets. Three pieces of advice: Don't trust her, don't turn your back on her, and don't ask her to hold your lead pipe for you while you take a nap in the conservatory. **B+**

Mr. Green

Mr. Green didn't do it. Do you know why? He didn't have the conejos! (Spanish for "rabbits." And I stand by that.) Mr. Green is a cigar-chomping, balding beef-jerky broker from Urbana, Illinois—it's obvious he doesn't know from murder. I could see him kicking a potted plant in a blind fit of pure glandular rage, but that's about it. **D**

Mrs. White

Mrs. White, having waited on Mr. Boddy hand, foot, and teakettle for untold years without complaint, is a prime candidate to have snapped like an autumn twig and offed him with any of the weapons that were lying around or, in a pinch, stabbed him in the back with one of the little red pegs from Battleship. Personally, I think "Clue II: The Wrath of Mrs. White" would make for great educational board-game fun for the whole family. **A−**

Professor Plum

A professor, yes, but what sort of professor? A detached academician in the tradition of the Professor from Gilligan's

Island? An evil genius, intellectual heir to Professor Moriarty? I actually see him as more in the vein of Dr. Bunsen Honeydew from the old *Muppet Show*; roundish, bumbling, and made of chartreuse felt. Man, I have to stop getting loaded on Buttershots before writing these things . . . **C**

BREAKFAST CEREALS

Cap'n Crunch with Crunchberries

What is a "Cap'n," anyway? The rank below a "Maj'r"? Anyhow, I am fully in favor of this cereal. Lovely does-not-occur-in-nature pink color to the crunchberries, extra points for pretending that they're actual fruit, neat spokescharacter. The only real flaw is that it seems to be specifically designed to scrape three layers of skin off your gums with each bowl. **A–**

Cookie Crisp

Lame. It was a good concept, it could have gone somewhere, but the fact is that the cereal bits bear no closer resemblance to chocolate chip cookies than Fruity Pebbles do to actual rocks. Also, this Cookie Crook character is shamelessly derivative of the whole Trix Rabbit Cereal Theft genre, only instead of the kids looking after their own damn cereal, they have an animated figure of authority to protect it for them. I am, however, an advocate of pouring milk on Chips Ahoy and eating that for breakfast. **C–**

Cocoa Puffs

The canonical chocolate sugar cereal. First off, it turns the milk chocolatey with eerie efficiency. When you've finished the cereal, that milk is damn chocolatey. Secondly, it actually does stay crunchy in milk. I don't know for how long, I haven't run tests, but its crunchy-staying power is remarkable. Thirdly, Sonny is a fine cartoon spokesanimal in the no-pants tradition. And finally, and this is the vital point, it's the only cereal that openly admits to inducing hyperactivity. "Go cuckoo for Cocoa Puffs" is obvious shorthand for "Parents, your children are going to be putting Keds marks on the walls after a couple bowls of this stuff." **A**

Honeycomb

In my childhood, the three main selling points of Honeycomb were: (a) The individual cereal pieces are about an inch in diameter, (b) they have a lot of surface area, and (c) large people will attempt to take it from you if you eat it. So, given these dubious advantages, it is unsurprising that I am somewhat disappointed with the cereal. I've also never been terribly fond of honey-flavored breakfast cereal ("The delicious corn and oat cereal that's been mugged with honey!"), so that was another point against. Still, it's the only cereal I know that actually improves in flavor when damp. **C**

Spider-Man Cereal

This one's relatively new, part of the continual march of tie-in cereals that appear on the market, make a few bucks, then fade away. Folks, they're not even trying with this one. The marshmallow bits are really sad. They don't look like anything. You read the side of the box, it explains what they are, and they *still* don't look like anything. The premium inside is a lame "trading card," and the cereal itself ("spider-webs") is just hexagonal frosted Rice Chex. Bleah. **D+**

Cinnamon Mini Buns

This is just not an exciting cereal. Let's face it, when you were a kid, Cinnamon Buns were just not as thrilling a breakfast sugar food as, say, doughnuts. So from the beginning you've got this "capture the tedium" feeling. Then there's the interesting discovery that when reduced to miniature size, cinnamon buns resemble some sort of tidepool mollusk. The box I got came with a little superhero comic book, so they're obviously trying to hit the kid market, but I think it's pretty well doomed from the beginning. **D**

THREE'S COMPANY CHARACTERS

Chrissy

Suzanne Somers just won't go away, will she? But before the Buttmaster, before the Thighmaster, before *The Suzanne Somers Show* and *She's the Sheriff*, there was Christmas "Chrissy" Snow, capturing the hearts and "minds" of the sort of people who found Marilyn Monroe movies too intellectual. Without her, the show would have been nothing more than a genteel sitting-room comedy of the type so loved by the Edwardian British, and indeed her departure signaled the beginning of the end for this lovable space that needs your face. And hey, how many women can claim to have single-handedly set the feminist movement back twenty years? **D+**

Janet

Where Chrissy taught us that you can be a bimbo and still rake in the bucks hawking dubious athletic equipment on infomercials, Janet provided the good news that being dark-haired and assertive doesn't mean you can't be treated like bargain-counter meat as well. In fact, one of the central messages of *Three's Company* is that everyone can get leered at in public. Except, perhaps, for Mr. Furley. But we'll get to him in a bit. **C**

Jack

Am I the only one who noticed that "Jack Tripper" is a sort of anagrammy acrostic thingie for "Jack T[he] Ripper"? One more subliminal gambit in the International Sitcom Conspiracy, but it gave the whole show a disturbing air, as if the season finale might involve a crawl space and the phrase "hunter of the Lord." Anyhow. Jack, I think, provided the only legitimate cultural truth in the series. To wit: If you can cook really well, you can get away with anything. **C+**

Larry

Wisecracking Mercutio to Jack's Romeo, philosophical Horatio to Jack's madcap Hamlet, Larry was an everyjerk who served the incredibly important purpose of making all the other sponge brains on the roster look good by comparison. I mean, let's face it, nobody on *Three's Company* is exactly a supernova of taste and charisma. By and large, they make the Sweathogs look like the cultural elite. Next to Larry, though, they blossom into borderline non-loserhood. **C+**

Mr. Furley

This must have been quite a stretch for Don Knotts, having to break out of his usual role of lemur-eyed backwater twit on the edge of an aneurysm to play a suburban, bandana-wearing, lemur-eyed twit on the edge of an aneurysm. I imagine there's probably a whole cohort of Roper partisans out there who see Furley as a landlord-come-lately, sort of a George Lazenby of bedroom farce, but Knotts is the one with the range. He's played a cartoon fish, for God's sake! A lemur-eyed cartoon fish on the edge of an aneurysm, to be fair, but still, I'd like to see Norman Fell try that one. **B−**

The Ropers

Who in the name of the Roman god of spin-offs thought that anyone wanted to see a half hour dedicated to these people? On the show they were passable second bananas, keeping comedic tensions high by threatening to toss Jack out on his corduroy-encased ass if he showed any signs of heterosexuality, but whatever meager laughs they contributed were due solely to their sheer awfulness. Take a completely repulsive couple, the male of which is constantly fending off sexual advances of the female, put them in their own show, and what do you get? Well, *Married with Children*, actually. All the more reason to abhor them. **D**

QUIZ:
ARE YOU A
ONE-HIT WONDER?

Yes No

☐ ☐ 1. Do three out of four lines from the chorus of your hit song contain a heretofore undiscovered euphemism for the sex act?

☐ ☐ 2. Do the lyrics contain the name of your band?

☐ ☐ 3. Are you fourteen years old?

☐ ☐ 4. Have you ever appeared on a Prince album?

☐ ☐ 5. Are you a "supergroup" made up of the members of previously successful bands who did not actually sing or write lyrics?

☐ ☐ 6. Are you a hard-core metal and/or punk band that decided for the hell of it to release a single in the style of a big-band tune, a children's song, or a rap song?

☐ ☐ 7. Is your song about dancing, even though you, yourself, cannot dance worth shit?

☐ ☐ 8. Is your song a wry comment on the state of the music industry?

☐ ☐ 9. Does the word "Beatles" appear anywhere in your press release, and you're not British?

☐ ☐ 10. Is your song a cover of a middle-of-the-road seventies hit, faithful except for the fact that you turn the distort on your guitars up to "2" and you sneer while singing it?

☐   ☐   11. Is your song a cover of a disaffected, ironic eighties hit, faithful except for the fact that it's played on an acoustic instrument and you sound very sincere?

☐   ☐   12. Are you Australian?

SCORING: Give yourself one point for each "yes."

0 points: Congratulations. You've got at least one more album to engineer a dive into obscurity.

1 point: This is probably it for your career until they start doing "00s flashbacks."

2–3 points: You'd better start working on burning out, because otherwise you'll be fading away very shortly.

4+ points: If you're a fourteen-year-old Australian who released a sensitive acoustic cover of "Video Killed the Radio Star," enjoy it while it lasts, kid, and get used to a life of pointing to the $1.99 bins and saying "Hey, that was me!"

CHRISTMAS SONGS

"Here Comes Santa Claus"

This is a blatant example of lazy songwriting. I mean, really, "Santa Claus Lane"? Where, exactly, is Santa Claus Lane? If your particular town doesn't have a Santa Claus Lane, does that mean Santa Claus can't come right down it, and children will wake up Christmas morning to find nothing but empty stockings and apologies? Or is it like a carpool lane, a special section of the freeway you can't drive unless you're a jolly old elf or are accompanied by a jolly old elf? Correct answer: They made it up, it sounds jaunty. **C–**

"Frosty the Snowman"

You know what I like about this song? It has an honest-to-Kringle sad ending. Doomed from the start, Frosty ends up melting like a Crayola on the dashboard, with only the promise that he'll come back again someday. It's the *Empire Strikes Back* of Christmas carols. **A–**

"Jingle Bell Rock"

I don't know where they get off calling this "rock." It's not even Jingle Bell Easy Listening. Not a great song in the first place, this is made even worse by its overinflated sense of hipness. I can just imagine some sixty-five-year-old crooner saying "And here's one the young people will enjoy." You want to hear a Christmas rock song? The Kinks, "Father Christmas," end of story. **D**

"The Chipmunk Song"

For me, the only appeal of the Chipmunks was in hearing hits of the eighties rendered in their electronically tortured little voices. (Which is not to say that most eighties pop stars didn't themselves have electronically tortured voices.) Given that, I fail to see why anyone would be interested in their original compositions. How do you explain Christ to a chipmunk, anyway? **D–**

"The Little Drummer Boy"

There's something charming about this, a song about the world's first drum solo. It also has a nice little lesson about how you should give whatever you can. Presumably if the drummer boy didn't have his drum, he would have given the newborn savior a little shadow-puppet show or something. Me, I would have just asked one of the wise men if I could put my name on his gift, too, and pay him back later. **B**

"My Favorite Things"

When did this become a Christmas song? I remember hearing this as part of the infuriatingly soothing mall lineup a few Christmases ago, and since then it's been a minor player in the carol scene. It has a couple of references to mittens and packages and the like, but it's hardly a seasonal song. Can't we all agree that the Christmas canon doesn't need adding to? If you're really getting tired of the usual songs—and who isn't?—learn "Fum Fum Fum" or "The Wassail Song" or something. **C–**

ASPECTS OF
THE MOVIE THEATER

Previews

What I don't understand is why they have maybe two guys, tops, doing the voice-overs for previews. Every preview has one of these two guys, except for the art flick previews with no voice-over, where they figure you'll be pulled in by a few quick shots of people ballroom dancing in period garb and a scene where an attractive person says "I have always believed . . . that life was for the living." Previews are fun, but can't we get some variety here? How about Casey Kasem? I'll go to any film with Casey Kasem doing the preview voice-over as long as there are no Klumps in it. **A–**

Ticket Takers

Apparently, there's a huge gulf of communication in the six steps between the box office and the actual door of the movie theater. The invention of the telegraph, the beeper, and the chat room have done nothing to bridge this gap, and a small slip of paper with the words "LETHL WPN 5" remains the only way to prove that you aren't trying to pull a fast one on United Artists. Still, no skin off my pancreas, and it keeps teenagers off the streets, wearing bow ties, and glowering at the masses. **C**

Food

The biggest change in the delicate balance between the public and the media conglomerates will come when they invent
a device like the metal-detecting wands they use in airports,
only this will detect candy bars. One wave of this thing and
suddenly alarms are going off and you're being relieved of
the bag of fun-size Snickers you had cleverly concealed in
your armpit. Will the moviegoing audience be reduced to
those actually willing to pay a 400 percent markup on
Gummi Bears, or will the public rise up against their
oppressors like the heroes of a painfully revisionist summer
historical drama? **C–**

Introductory Snippet

The little poorly focused, scratch-covered computer animation at the beginning of the screening telling you to shut the
hell up informs no one. It's like a PSA for movie clods. The
guy talking in a normal tone of voice about his upcoming
foosball tourney has obviously made a conscious personal
choice to be a dick. He's probably the same guy who parks
his SUV right on top of the line because he figures you
should get one parking space for every 25K you spend on
your vehicle. **D**

Posters

This seems like a pretty recent (circa Gump) development,
but these days every wannabe blockbuster has a poster that
goes up maybe a year before release, attempting to raise
interest in a movie with an obscure tag line like "In Summer
2003, You Will Learn Not to Burn." The main people
excited by a poster like this are those who know what the
hell it's talking about, which tend to be those who have
scoured the Web and already know the plot and the plots
for the two planned sequels, but it's nice to have the appearance of anticipation, at least. **A**

The Credits

What I want is a Web page that tells you, with no spoilers, whether to stay for the credits. I have friends who want to sit through the credits no matter what, even if it's an animated movie that has twenty-five people listed for every character, including Blinko the Disoriented Ferret, but the only reason I stay is because sometimes there are outtakes. Burgess Meredith coming up with thirty different crude ways to say "have sex," bless my ankles that's entertainment to make even the most saturnine frat boy smile. **C**

THANKSGIVING FOODS

Turkey

When you get right down to it, turkey is not a bad choice for a feast holiday. Turkeys are low-fat, reasonably gigantic, and they make good cartoon characters for holiday specials. What cracks me up is the supposed scientific finding that gets bandied about this time of year that says that turkey contains a chemical that makes you sleepy, as if the people who had ham instead are out roller-blading after dinner. When you consume your weight in buttered foodstuffs, you're going to feel a bit nappish, turkey or no turkey. **B+**

Canned Cranberry Sauce

There are many excellent uses for cranberries and cranberry juice, many of them involving vodka. However, the canned tribute to the gods of pectin that gets served at many Thanksgiving tables pretty much leeches the appeal right out of the suckers. Look at it this way: When was the last time you heard anyone say "Boy, we should have bought more canned cranberry sauce," or "Yay! There's leftover canned cranberry sauce!" Now, I'm sure there are many people out there who are saying to themselves "Ay! The canned cranberry sauce is my favorite part of Thanksgiving!" These people are perverts. **D**

Candied Yams

Interestingly enough, studies I just made up show that your average person does not, except on Thanksgiving, eat (a) anything candied, or (b) anything made of yams. I imagine the Yam Council and the Candification Board are working hard to change this, but I have a better idea for increasing candied yam awareness: Make the phrase a slang term for the gonad portion of the male anatomy. Think about it. The increase in groin humor in the movies and television has created an ever increasing need for euphemisms for same, and if I can contribute even a single line to a *Mighty Ducks* sequel, I can die a happy man. **B–**

Pumpkin Pie

This is, without question, the most noble thing you can do with a gourd, and it's among the most pleasurable. I have childhood memories of my mother transforming our Halloween pumpkin into our Thanksgiving pumpkin pies, which is heartwarming and all until you realize that carved pumpkins start to look pretty grotesque by Veterans Day, so I'm hoping this is just part of the same false memory syndrome that led me to believe that my father invented the cheeseburger in 1975. Anyhow, pumpkin pie. Good stuff. **A**

Mashed Potatoes

This is one of the two essential Thanksgiving items that actually gets eaten throughout the year, the other being bread. I really dig on mashed potatoes. I would love to travel back in time and shake the hand of the man or woman who invented mashed potatoes, in spite of the very real risk that I'd end up shattering the flow of time, making it so that my parents never met, invalidating my own existence and creating a temporal rift that would result in a world where ficus trees rule the earth. And then I'd do the same thing with the person who invented garlic mashed potatoes. **A+**

Stuffing

Another sign of the holidays are the cheery warnings in the food section of your local newspaper that tell you that if you cook your stuffing inside the turkey, you may as well put a sign in your upper intestine saying "Evil Bacteria Wanted. Toxic Biological By-products a Plus." Apparently, in spite of the fact that turkeys need to be cooked in a hot oven for hours, this isn't enough to stop stuffing bacteria, which kill three billion people every year. So if you live in one of the states that still allows internally cooked stuffing, you can add a certain adventurous quality to your holiday meal by defying the odds and blazing your own flavored bread trail. **B**

HAIR PRODUCTS

Hair Color

I colored my hair once. There's this stuff called Manic Panic, also known as "Club Kid in a Jar," which allows you to turn your hair interesting colors, then wash it out the next day, unless you're me. First off, my hair was supposed to be black, and it turned shoe polish–brown instead. It was supposed to wash out, but it turned my hair a subtle shade of moss green that would have been very attractive covering my couch instead of my scalp. So I'm not a big fan. **C–**

Shampoo

You could just use soap, you know, but that would prevent your hair from looking like a movie star's. The first thing big-shot Hollywood producers do when they make someone a movie star is give them the secret shampoo. You can't get it, of course, but the less you spend on shampoo, the further you are from the secret formula. For every ten bucks you spend on a bottle, shampoo makers are allowed to put one movie star ingredient in there. There are a *lot* of secret ingredients. **B**

Conditioner

I'm not sure I want my hair conditioned. Isn't that what they do to lab rats to make them fear pictures of Jeeps or whatever? My particular favorite conditioners are those designed to make your hair better able to withstand the torture of being permed. I like the skewed logic of selling you stuff to protect your hair from the godawful crap you're doing to it. It's like marketing "Extra-Padded Slap Yourself Gloves." **B–**

Creme Rinse

Isn't conditioner creme rinse? Or is creme rinse conditioner? This proliferation of stuff you're supposed to massage into your braincase is one reason I shave my head. (The other was getting my hair in my mouth during sex. You know how it is.) I once saw a bottle of "body building creme rinse," which I can only assume makes your hair more muscular. **D+**

Gel

Hair gel reached the height of popularity in the eighties, when both hard styling and translucent liquids were all the rage. Gel still retains the mark of this era, with the super-heroish superlatives used to describe how well it keeps your hair from moving in a high wind. Extra Control! Mega Hold! Ultra Firm! Together, they are: the Legion of Hair Gels! **B+**

INTERNAL ORGANS

Heart

The ancient-but-silly Greeks believed that the heart was the seat of intelligence and emotion, because it beats faster when you feel strong emotion and because you die when a ninja rips it out of your chest. Of course, now we're much more enlightened and we know that the heart serves only as a handy storage area for saturated fats and as something for people to grab at in feigned astonishment. **C**

Lungs

I know that it's become all the rage for antismoking demonstrations to include a diseased lung being slapped on the table, but let's be honest with ourselves: A healthy lung ain't exactly Renoir, either. In fact, slap pretty much any random hunk of disembodied flesh on the table and say "See? This is what will happen to you if you start smoking: a perfectly healthy goat kidney!" and get the same effect. **B**

Stomach

My intensive studies of the stomach have determined that it is perfectly smooth, almost cartoonish, and that it appreciates having computer-generated fluorescent liquid being introduced into it, so much so, in fact, that it will often glow an angry red if it doesn't get these liquids. Thanks again, television commercials! **C**

Brain

The most important thing about the brain is that you become much, much more intelligent if it's showing. If you can arrange to have it encased in a transparent dome, or to have it imprinting itself on a soft membrane that you have in place of a skull, you're pretty much ready to create elaborate laser cannons and mindless zombie slave creatures. Remember that the next time you have to take a test and have access to a band saw. **A**

Spleen

I'm not going to point out the actual function of the spleen, because its major appeal is in the low-level mystery created by the fact that most people don't really care about it one way or the other. It's just this floppy mass of tissue that's fun to say and lives within each one of us, kind of like a guardian angel made of Silly Putty. **A–**

SEXUAL POSITIONS

Missionary Position

It's fun that the word "missionary" has come to indicate both those who spread the word of God and men who fuck with their asses in the air. In spite of the unsavory association with propriety, the good old "MisPo" is actually quite convenient for those times when you don't want to worry about equilibrium. It probably wouldn't have such a vanilla reputation if it weren't such a poor angle for explicit filming. **A–**

Woman on Top

It is said, mostly by students at liberal universities looking for ways to introduce sex into the conversation, that Adam's first wife, Lilith, was kicked out of the Garden of Eden for insisting that she be on top during those first bouts of paradisiacal boinking. Supposedly, this was some symbolic power struggle, but hey, if I can advance the cause of women's equality by lying back and letting the woman do the lingam boogie, I'm glad to be of service. **A+**

Sixty-nine

Fun, at least for a change of pace, but I like to be able to concentrate on what I'm doing, you dig? Mutual simultaneous oral attention is like opening presents and blowing out candles at the same time. And then there's the giggle-fest after phrases like "Class, turn your books to page sixty-nine." Still, it is fun to race each other, however you define the finish line. **C–**

Rear Entry

This really needs a better name. "Rear entry" sounds like a tarnished aluminum sign in an alleyway, and "Doggie style" brings up unfortunate images of—no surprise—dogs humping. Probably the best is "from behind," although experts agree that your better sexual descriptors don't start with prepositions. Anyhow. Fun, but on a smooshy bed it offers endless opportunities for toppling over like a drunk on a bar stool. A naked, thrusting drunk. **C+**

Standing

Oh, please. As graceful as this might look in "The Illustrated Kama Sutra," it requires the balance of a gymnast, the thigh muscles of a ballet dancer, the build of the Rolling Stones circa 1968, and a partner closer in height than I, at six foot four, am likely to encounter. **D**

BEVERAGE CONTAINERS

Massive Plastic Containers

It's only the covenant of the rainbow that allays my fears that one day all of humanity will drown in a deluge caused by a spilt large soda from a very competitive convenience store. When you have to start adding multiple adjectives to "big," you know your drinks are larger than any sane person requires. Even better are the ones that taper down like an ice cream cone so that they ostensibly can fit in your car's beverage holder. This would work really well if my car's beverage holder extended two feet from the dash and was reinforced with flying buttresses. **D+**

Cans

The disappointment of curbside recycling is that there is no longer any need to crush the cans down into sad little disks so that they'll all fit in the back of the pickup when you go on your annual trip to the recycling center to exchange five hundred pounds of aluminum for approximately eight cents. They're still light and flexible enough to throw at offensively stupid commercials without damaging your television, though, so I'm okay with them. **C+**

Bottles

I have recently noticed billboards advertising beer in plastic bottles because, and I'm paraphrasing here, you are a drunk asshole who can't hold on to a simple long-neck. I can't complain about this, mostly because you are, but I think it's amusing that they finally admitted it. The first guy who forgets this when getting in one of those bar fights where you break off the bottom of your beer bottle is going to look pretty silly, though. Boing! **B**

Styrofoam Cups

Styrofoam cups are forever linked in my mind with crappy bank coffee and powdered nonorganic creamer. Which is where they belong. Styrofoam cups just feel wrong, as if someone distilled chalk-squeaking and piss-shiver into physical form and stacked it next to the decaf. **D**

Paper Cups

I've heard far too many arguments about whether it's worse to deforest continents or bury them in nondecomposing plastic by virtue of your cup choice, so I'm going to assume it's a wash and judge paper cups purely on the grounds of utility. Paper cups are good because they can be made into crafts easily and because some of them have riddles printed on them. **B–**

QUIZ:
EITHER/OR

1. Pirates like to keep their treasure in:
   ☐ Your ass
   ☐ A hole in the ground
2. You walk into a biker bar and start pontificating loudly about the superiority of Vespas. What does a large man named Rottweiler get medieval on?
   ☐ Your ass
   ☐ A hole in the ground
3. Bugs Bunny likes to pop up out of:
   ☐ Your ass
   ☐ A hole in the ground
4. In *Superman: The Movie*, General Zod says something that sounds suspiciously like "You will bow down before me, Jor-El! Both you, and then one day . . ."
   ☐ "Your ass!"
   ☐ "A hole in the ground!"
5. One of the biggest attractions in America's national parks is a place where at regular intervals huge plumes of water shoot out of:
   ☐ Your ass
   ☐ A hole in the ground
6. Your neighbor asks you how he can be more right-eous. Paraphrasing Exodus 20, you tell him he can keep his mitts off of:
   ☐ Your ass
   ☐ A hole in the ground

ANSWERS:

1, 3, 5:   A hole in the ground
2, 4, 6:   Your ass

SCORING: Give youself one point for each correct answer.

0–3 points: You seem to lack a firm grasp of either your
              ass or ground holes. However, this is not a
              problem in many job markets.

4–5 points: You seem to have a general idea of the
              differences and similarities between your
              ass and a hole in the ground, but we
              suggest you spend some time studying and
              comparing them for future reference.

6 points: Congratulations. You have mastered vital
              gluteal-excavation discernment skills.

DVD EXTRAS

Letterbox

I am not a purist. I do not have Dolby Surround sound with a bass speaker implanted in my lower intestine. I do not have an S-Video adapter for my Game Boy. But wide-screen movies presented in pan-and-scan, particularly those that feature long conversations between disembodied noses on either side of the screen, bug the hell out of me. I don't know why they always made VHS movies in this abominative format, but if at some point the Marketing Cabal decides that the public prefers DVD movies in pan-and-scan, I'm tossing out my player and going back to making up stories about happy bunnies in my head. **A**

Multiple Languages

Rainy-day activity: Rent or buy the DVD of *Viva Las Vegas*, the best movie ever to feature Ann-Margret explaining the origins of the Hoover Dam, and turn on French dubbing with English subtitles. Suddenly this fluffy Elvis romp is transformed into a sophisticated and urbane French farce suitable for discussing over espresso drinks! That, my friends, is the magic of multiple languages. **B+**

Director's Commentary

When I first bought my DVD player, I was disappointed every time I rented a movie that didn't have director's commentary. It didn't take me long to realize that most movies simply aren't worth running discussion that lasts as long as the movie itself. I hear that the *Dungeons and Dragons* DVD has director's commentary on it. If the commentary track isn't made up entirely of tearful, pleading apologies, I don't want to hear it. **C–**

Multiple Views

Some have prophesied that DVDs will allow viewers to take the place of directors and film editors, finally putting the power of cinema in the hands of the so-called common man. They are right, as long as you substitute "pornography" for "cinema" and "hand" for "hands." Multiple views in mainstream films have mostly been limited to reverse angles of lovable St. Bernards in one or two scenes, but there are porn titles that promise to let you orchestrate your own orgy without having to make sure the cast has enough body oil and depilatories. **C–**

Interactive Menus

Most DVD cases showcase lists of exciting features on the back, and most of those lists include "interactive menus" as a selling point. This is the equivalent of advertising that the disc will cause your TV to emit *real photons*. Even the crummiest deceptively named documentary about the *Titanic* has interactive menus. For that matter, what would a noninteractive menu be in this context? A list of scenes from an entirely different movie? **D**

COLD SYMPTOMS

Sneezing

In minute quantities, sneezes can be gratifying. I've heard orgasms described as a sort of full-body sneeze, and that's an alarmingly accurate description. I don't go on the Internet at two in the morning looking for pictures of bee pollen, so I think I've still got perspective, but I figure if you're going to be expelling mucus at fastball speeds, you may as well put it in the best possible light. **B+**

Stuffy Nose

When I was younger I didn't realize that sinuses actually swell when you're sick. I thought that the reason I couldn't breathe out of at least one nostril was that a wad of passage-blocking snot was in the way, and it bugged the preteen *hell* out of me that no amount of blowing could clear it. The only good thing about a stuffy nose is that if you're in too much misery to sleep, you can always play "waiting for the nostril switch." **D+**

Coughing

The human animal has an astonishing repertoire of coughs, the sickness equivalent of a high-end synth box. My favorite, which is to say the least annoying, is a quick lung-clearing hack. The worst are those long resonant vibrating coughs that leave you feeling as if your lungs had been scrubbed by an obsessive-compulsive with a fresh scouring pad. **C–**

Fever

I don't find fevers pleasant—except, of course, for disco fever—but I am grateful for them as the ultimate vindication of one's whining, short of wasting death. Complaining about headaches and scratchy throats can be dismissed as a ploy to get attention and/or avoid work, but once that thermometer reads 98.7 or so, you're sick, baby, with all the pillow-fluffing and daytime-television-watching due thereto. **B–**

Sore Throat

A vague scratching at the back of my throat is, often as not, the first sign of an oncoming attack of several days of burning misery. Because of this, I pay frequent low-level attention to my throat, the way adolescent girls pay frequent low-level attention to the growth of their breasts. Unfortunately, it's very easy to convince yourself that you have a minor sore throat if you've just woken up, inhaled cold air, or eaten wasabi in the last week, so there are a lot of false alarms, and many oranges have given up their lives for my paranoia. **D–**

Headache

I don't get many headaches, of which I'm glad, because if one is to believe television advertisements, most headaches are slightly more painful than extended torture by intelligent evil mandrills and are accompanied by such uncomfortable effects as blurry close-ups of you grimacing while holding a hand to your forehead. Luckily, you've got Epoxidril, with the maximum amount of painkiller available without immediate liver failure. **D**

"PAUL IS DEAD" CLUES

The Walrus Is an Ancient Viking Symbol for Death

Oh, please. Can you imagine a bunch of Vikings coursing their way through the frigid Nordic waters, looking into the dense fog with trepidation beginning to form across their brows, when suddenly one of them sees: The Black Walrus! The Walrus of Death! That Undiscovered Walrus from Whose Bourne No Traveler Returns! It sounds distinctly Pythonesque. **C–**

The Green Apple on the LP Turns Bloodred Underwater

This is astoundingly cool, except for the bit where it's a complete lie. When I first heard this one, I leapt up to test it and ended up with nothing more than a wet *Abbey Road*. For the record, it doesn't work on CDs, either, and you really don't want to try it on 8-tracks. Still, if some musician out there perfects the technology to turn a green apple blood-red on an LP underwater, I swear right here that I will buy your album, no matter how bad it is. **C+**

"Lovely Rita" Refers to Paul's Car Crash

The theory here is that Paul's fatal car accident was caused by him being distracted by an attractive meter maid at an inopportune moment. Boy, those mop tops are gruesome, aren't they? Not only do they plant various lyrical clues referring to heads flying off and teeth flying out and hair catching on fire, they go ahead and write an entire song devoted to the agent of Paul's untimely demise. Makes Nick Cave look like "Peter, Paul, and Mommy" by comparison. **C**

The Drum on *Sgt. Pepper* Spells Out "HE DIE" If You Use a Mirror

Ooh! Spooky! And unlike the Blood Apple, this one actually works. Oh, sure, what it spells looks more like | ONE | X HE | DIE, but the "HE DIE" is in there, which can be quite unnerving if it's night and you've been reading about severed heads and disembodied teeth for a couple of hours. **B+**

I Buried Paul

I'm led to understand that the second Beatles Anthology album proves once and for all that John was in fact singing "cranberry sauce," which alone is a good enough reason to spend thirty bucks on a bunch of songs you've heard before. What remains unanswered, however, is the question of what the hell did he mean by "cranberry sauce"? Do British people even eat cranberry sauce? I thought it was a uniquely American dish, consumed once a year as penance for slavery and inventing the sitcom. It's a mystery wrapped in an enigma and digitally remastered. **B**

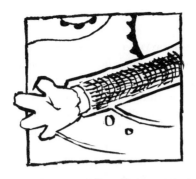

ASPECTS OF THE WEATHER REPORT

Humidity Index

While I appreciate the attempt to give me a context for my misery, I find the calculation of how hot it *feels* like to be less than useful. First off, it's wrong. When it's 95 degrees in California, I don't think "Hey, this is just like 85 degrees in Nashville in July." I'm just glad I'm not there. I think that the weatherfolk should at least attempt to be more evocative. "It's ninety-two degrees, but it *feels* like you're being stuffed fully clothed into a sauna and made to breathe through a wet sock." **D**

Fronts

Another thing I appreciate about weatherpersons is their cheerful crusade to educate me. "There's a warm front coming in off this high-pressure area in the north, and it's running into a cold front *here*, and you know what that means!" says the weatherman. "Locusts?" I venture. "Thunderstorms!" says the weatherman. "Well, you could have just *said* that," I reply. Then I throw a sock at the screen. **C**

Forecast Diagrams

Once upon a memory, the forecast was simple and stationary. You had your sun and your clouds. The clouds could rain or snow. Maybe you'd see the word "wind" if there was a ratings battle going on. The local all-weather station now has animated weather that, I think, is supposed to provide a sense of time, so that if there are clouds on the left side of the Monday box but not on the right, that means Monday will start out cloudy and clear up. And if it's night, the "next few hours" forecast has a moon. The clouds actually go behind the moon, so it's not strictly meteorologically accurate, but points for trying. **C+**

Temperature Bands

I think of this as the "envy and spite" chart. With one sweeping glance, you can see that Oregon is having a nicer day than you are, but at least you're not in Missouri. It's especially easy for me, because as far as my Nordic blood is concerned, blue is good. Some people prefer living in the light yellow areas, but my gaze is always drawn longingly toward Canada. **B**

Lightning Charts

One of the nice maps they go through on the Weather Channel is the chart of every single lightning strike, usually displayed in this shimmering band of plus and minus signs like an arithmetic book breaking into a riot. I'm sure they have some miraculous satellite that keeps track of these things, but I'd still like to have the job of standing on my porch looking for strikes and counting "one one-hundred, two one-hundred, three one-hundred . . ." **B–**

Sweeping Arm Movements

What I want for my birthday is this: a tape of weather reports without the superimposed maps. Just a man or lady standing in front of a blue screen, staring off-camera, babbling about high-pressure areas and making sweeping arm movements. I think that would be *hilarious.* The sweeping arm movements would really make it for me. **B**

AQUATIC MAMMALS

Otters

If we enter the fourth millennium in a world where the only remaining vertebrates are adorable, we should call it "The Sea Otter Effect," after these creatures, which would have been tragically wiped out if not for the fact that they roll over and expose their bellies when they eat. The Monterey Bay Aquarium, where they put on otter feedings, likes to emphasize that these are wild carnivores with teeth that could earn you a nickname having to do with the number of your fingers, but tell that to the piles of plush, shell-grasping otter toys. **B+**

Manatees

If cute animals are the ones that end up with the most environmental protectors, how do you explain the drive to save the manatee? My guess is that the cause of their demise—getting slashed into gobbets by boat propellors—is even more gruesome than their appearance. As a society, I think we want to preserve manatees because we don't want our children to have to hear about deep bleeding manatee lacerations in nature classes. **C−**

Whales

If anything good is to come out of the current obsession with preserving copyright in the face of reckless sharing and unauthorized campfire strumming, it's that perhaps the whales themselves will see some of the cash piled up from sales of whale-song albums. Then the cetacean world will have its own Britney Spears, who can pay fishermen not to kill it for valuable oil and perfume ingredients, just like Britney did. **B+**

Dolphins

It's a testament to the beauty and grace of dolphins that they can be so breathtaking in spite of unfortunate associations with hoop jumping, football, and overpriced crystal sculptures. I once saw a school of dolphins migrating off the coast of California, their black dorsal fins breaking the surf and shining in the sun, so graceful and perfect that I could ignore the people around me who felt the phrase "Hey, look, dolphins!" could not be repeated too many times. **A**

Walruses

I think it's time to dispel the many hurtful stereotypes that have come to be associated with walruses. Firstly, not all of them are named "Wally." Many are named "Walter" or "Wilbur." Secondly, they haven't worn waistcoats or watch fobs since approximately 1912. Thirdly, they do not lower property values if they move in next door. Thank you. **C**

PINBALL FEATURES

Tilt Sensors

I hate to sound like a pigeon-feeding old man, but all these flashy Final Fantasy Mario Solid Gear Tekken Wars video computer games lack one of the simple joys in life: facing a pinball game with nothing on your side but physics, flippers, and a willingness to shove that fucker around like a sumo wrestler. I don't mind tilt sensors, but I did mind that one arcade where the attendant threatened to throw me out for bumping a pinball game. The hell? That's like being kicked out of the bumper cars for not signaling. **C**

Bumpers

Having established myself as old-school, I have to admit a weakness for pinball games with ramps and moving targets and dancing plastic guys and such. Particularly nice for this is the Street Fighter pinball game where you get to beat up a car and make an acrobatic young lady do cartwheels, and the Star Wars pinball game with a little plastic Death Star to blow up. In the face of all this whizz-crackery, plain old regular bumpers are a bit of a snooze. You shoot the ball up, it goes *whackity-whackity-whack* like a street-corner percussionist for a couple of seconds, and it comes down again. **C**

Ramps

Ramps are an integral part of the modern (i.e., post-1975) pinball game, but they make playing a poorly maintained game about as fun as playing Slinky on a football field. Often as not, the flippers wear out until they exert all the force of a newborn gerbil, and your best chance to get a ball up the ramp is to fall into a coma and dream happily of a world where all the pinball machines work perfectly while your immediate family decides whether to pull out your feeding tube. **A**

Plunger

The lamest development in pinball technology outside of that one arcade attendant I mentioned is the substitution of a large glowing button for the plunger. You just press the button and the ball bounces into play with a complete lack of finesse and subtlety. I can understand not wanting to have to replace a valuable two-cent spring every three years, but it removes some of the essential pinballness of the game and reduces us to the level of machines, rather than the level of people who swear at machines. **A**

Pop-Up Targets

My favorite kind of pop-up targets are the kind that spell things. You know, you play the Senate Floor Debate pinball game and you have to spell out "FILI BUST ER" on the various target banks to light the "override veto" ramp, that sort of thing. But maybe that's just because I like hurting letters. **C+**

WAYS TO CARRY THINGS

Fanny Pack

Everyone looks stupid in a fanny pack. It even somehow makes sleek, lean runners look like grannies perusing the ceramic candy dishes in a thrift shop. You'd think the name would tip people off, but no, the things are more popular than ever among those needing someplace to stash a disposable camera or a sports drink. **D–**

Purses

On one hand, purses seem like a wonderful idea. Throw it over one shoulder and you've got a place to keep tissues, a checkbook, chapstick, moist towelettes, feminine products (assuming you're feminine), interesting dried bones, Band-Aids, finger puppets, and whatever it is you like to put teeth marks on when you're nervous. The downside is that I've spent most of my adult life explaining that what I'm carrying is a "satchel," dammit. **B**

Clutches

This, on the other hand, seems like a colossally bad idea. If I'm understanding correctly, you put several items of great value into a little package that you have to cling to every second. It's like those baby things they put you through in high school where you have to take care of an egg so that you don't fuck other students, only you have to do it while wearing heels and yelling above a bad house band. **C–**

Backpacks

This would seem to be a perfect solution to my satchel/purse dilemma, but backpacks remind me too much of elementary school, unless they're actual hiking-around-style backpacks, in which case they remind me that I'm really busy this weekend and couldn't possibly go camping. **C–**

Wallets

Wallets are nice. Billfolds are even better. Having to carry a wad of paper, plastic, and glossy coupons the size of a guinea pig around in my back pocket makes me feel like the proud owner of an ass tumor, so I try to keep my wallet to a slim minimum. ATM card, AAA card, such credit cards as banks were foolish enough to offer me, driver's license with "gut me for spare organs" authorization, and ways to prove I deserve health care and video rentals, and that's it. That and a bill clip with enough cash to make me feel like a big, big man. **A**

QUIZ:
WHAT KIND OF
PERSONALITY QUIZ
TAKER ARE YOU?

1. You're taking a personality quiz on a bus when you reach your destination. What do you do?
   a) Get off the bus, then stand at the bus stop and finish the quiz before you go on with your day.
   b) Stash the quiz for finishing later.
   c) Leave the quiz on the bus, stuff it away, who cares? I was just killing time.
   d) Forage for insects and larvae to eat.

2. You come across a personality quiz in a magazine in your dentist's office, with several answers circled. What do you do?
   a) Look for a different personality quiz with no answers circled. After all, I wouldn't want my responses to be influenced by the person before me.
   b) Take the quiz. Who cares what someone else answered?
   c) Look around for *Highlights for Children*.
   d) Raise young in small collectives, with little concern for actual parentage of the cubs.

3. You've found a new "special person" in your life, but he or she doesn't like taking personality quizzes. What do you do?

   a) Dump this person. Anyone who doesn't understand personality quizzes doesn't understand me.

   b) Live with it. I don't need someone else's validation to take personality quizzes, and maybe with time we can take them together.

   c) Continue seeing him or her. There are more important things than personality quizzes.

   d) Live in the savannahs of southern or eastern Africa.

4. Your favorite magazine publishes a "special" theme issue that, for some reason, has no personality quizzes in it. What do you do?

   a) Write a letter to the editor demanding an explanation and a credit for the price of the issue.

   b) Pick up an issue of another, similar magazine that *does* have a personality quiz.

   c) Enjoy whatever the publisher put in instead of a personality quiz.

   d) Raise the hair on my mane and emit an unpleasantly musky fluid from my anal glands when threatened.

5. You take a personality quiz and it says you're a much less nice person than you think you are. What do you do?

   a) Accept its pronouncement and resolve to improve myself. After all, if it weren't accurate, it wouldn't have been published.

   b) Don't worry about it too much, as long as other personality quizzes assure me that I'm an okay person in other ways.

c) Nothing in particular. I don't take the analysis of someone who has never met me very seriously.

d) Use the abandoned burrow of another animal for my den.

SCORING: Count the number of "a," "b," "c," and "d" answers.

Mostly "a" answers:

You are a Personality Quiz Purist. You take your personality quizzes very seriously and don't let anything come between you and them.

Mostly "b" answers:

You are a Personality Quiz Pollyanna. You always look on the bright side of your personality quiz experience and don't let anything reduce your enjoyment.

Mostly "c" answers:

You are a Personality Quiz Pooper. You don't care about personality quizzes at all, for some reason.

Mostly "d" answers:

You are an aardwolf.

PIZZA TOPPINGS

Extra Cheese

Extra cheese? If you need extra cheese on your pizza, either (a) the pizza service you patronize is made up of a bunch of skimping dairy misers and you should find yourself another pizza source, or (b) your dietary needs would be better served by simply eating a bowl of hot cheese. **C–**

Pepperoni

Violently, tragically overrated. I'm convinced that the pepperoni tradition was begun by early pizza guys who wanted to foist the cheap, vile sausage off on the unknowing early pizza patrons, saving the good stuff for cute girls and especially heart-wrenching urchins. **C**

Sausage

Now this is a meat topping. If you get it at a good place, which is to say a place where you can distinguish the pizza crust from the refrigerator magnet that came with it, it can be a truly rich and rewarding food experience. And if not, it still beats the hell out of the bright-red grease saucers they call pepperoni. **B**

Pesto

Are you ready for pesto? Can you handle pesto? I've seen strong men crumble before a good pesto pizza, begging and drooling to be allowed another bite! Writhing in the torture of pure basil ecstasy! You're afraid, aren't you? You fear pesto! Bastard! Coward! Bastard! **A–**

Little Red Pepper Flakes

Man, I love these. You know, the ones in the big shake-jar next to the Parmesan powder? You shake them all over your pizza slice and they taste like an invading pizza army. It's like eating pizza sacked by Ostrogoths. **B**

Anchovies

Let's give fish particles their due, shall we? They're not really very good tasting, but they serve the dual purposes of being a funny topping and being the topping nobody orders. Say you're telling a joke, and the guy in the joke orders a pizza. Just put anchovies on the pizza and it doubles the comedy if it's a pretty pathetic joke in the first place. As for the second point, the fact is that there has to be one topping that nobody orders, and if there weren't anchovies, the entire Canadian bacon market would vanish and Canada itself would collapse into ruin, forcing us to send them billions of dollars in aid just to keep the For Better or for Worse cartoons coming. **B+**

AIR FRESHENERS

Car Air Fresheners

I once bought one of these—what can I say, my car was old and I enjoyed "Repo Man"—and boy, did it stink up the place. As much as I enjoyed the retro-lamo effect of a flat tree hanging from my rearview mirror, I learned a harsh lesson: Sinus-flensing clouds of pine scent are never hip. **D**

Plug-In Air Fresheners

These are just the dumbest thing. As I write this, California is playing a statewide game of electrical peek-a-boo because of a power shortage, and yet people are still inventing new things to plug into the wall for no apparent reason. What's next, gas-powered lip gloss? **D**

Baking Soda

The thing I love about baking soda is the number of times it's been near to the only thing in my freezer, nobly and uncomplainingly keeping its little lightless cubicle free of the scent of half a bag of frozen french fries and half a bottle of vodka. Rock on, little baking soda box. **A**

Potpourri

From the French, literally meaning "rotting pot." The irony here is that in many communal housing situations potpourri is used to cover the scent of both rotting things and pot. I can't say that I've ever found it particularly effective, mostly because the potpourri in question usually dates from about 1982, but at least it gives knickknack stores something to sell besides crystal pegasi and ceramic cherubs. **B–**

Aerosol Spray

It seems to me that "fresh air" is a pretty unambiguous phrase and that a mini-tempest of lemon scent doesn't qualify, but who am I to argue with a cadre of nameless commercial housewives? Perhaps it's only the vile effluvia of industrialization that keeps our atmosphere from smelling like a spilled bottle of off-brand sour mix. If so, however, viva la effluvia! **C–**

PLAGUES OF EGYPT

Frogs

Normally, you wouldn't expect a plague of frogs to convince Pharaoh to let the cat out, much less free thousands of slaves, but imagine this: You wake up one morning, get out of bed, and—*splorch*—step on a frog. Freshly dead amphibian ichor between your toes first thing in the morning. Pretty icky, huh? **B**

Locusts

Not bad. Locusts are horrid little insects, plus they eat crops. It's two great plagues that plague great together. One wonders, though, if the frogs ate locusts or if the two plagues had a truce, like that time G.I. Joe and Cobra had to team up to fight a common enemy. Didn't think I'd be able to work eighties cartoon shows into this one, did you? **A–**

Blood

A river of blood. Creepy. But in the end it sounds better than, say, a river of motor oil, syringes, and abandoned shopping carts. At least blood is organic. Still, I can see how when you've got a majorly river-based economy going, it could be difficult to make a transition to a massive blood-flow economy. **B+**

Hail

This is about when you realize you really are dealing with God and not just tough luck and weird weather patterns. Hail, okay, fine, you just do the ancient Egyptian equivalent of rolling up the car windows. But fire and hail in tandem is a big-ass clue that perhaps you're dealing with the chosen people and maybe you should just let them go and build your own damn stone monuments. **C**

Death of Cattle

It's pretty tough to rationalize what the cattle did to deserve the celestial smackdown. But admittedly that's a revisionist, post-*Babe* take on the situation. The Big Guy was never big on animal rights, what with the scapegoats and fatted calves and such. He am that He am, pardner, cows or no cows. **D+**

THE REST OF THE
PLAGUES OF EGYPT

Vermin

Might have been lice, might have been gnats, but I doubt that the Egyptians were worried about genus and species. "Gosh, I wonder what exact breed of insect is clogging my nostrils?" is not a question you hear very often. That's what I like about Passover seders: They're about the only time you're encouraged to discuss insect infestations at the dinner table. **B–**

Boils

Good one! Pus-filled sores are a too often overlooked tool in shaping social policy. If state governments were constitutionally allowed to visit horrible skin afflictions on, say, schools that performed below testing standards, I bet we'd soon have graduating classes that shamed even those darned Europeans with their hoity-toity math skills and their multilanguage fluency and their grasp of geography. **A**

Beasts

Apparently, this is kind of a tricky translation. The King James Bible has "flies," one translated Torah I found has "insects," but *A Rugrats Passover* has it as "wild beasts," so wild beasts it is. Wild beasts make me think of Tarzan, so I can't help but imagine a scene with Moses pounding his chest and emitting a jungle yodel, followed by a stampede of elephants and baboons and panthers and, I dunno, toucans and stuff coming down on Pharaoh and his buddies. It's not easy living in my head. **B**

Darkness

You know, after boils, locusts, dead farm animals, hail, and other assorted miseries, you'd think not having to look at your ravaged environs would actually be relatively relaxing. On the other hand, three days of not being able to do anything but sit around and converse about how much it sucks to be hated by God must have hastened the freeing process somewhat. **C–**

Death of the Firstborn

Hey. Way uncool. But then, it's the Old Testament: Much of the OT is taken up with the Creator coming down on group C for what group A did to group B. Think of all the llamas that died in the Flood! Is there any indication that the llamas had become insolent and cruel? Was God dissatisfied with their performance as llamas? No! But all of them except two took the big swim along with the human beings who were the problem in the first place. It's all part of God's pre-Christ oeuvre. But that doesn't mean I have to like it. **D–**

FORMS OF GAMBLING

Roulette

Roulette is the game of choice for people who want to lose money quickly. Betting on a single number is like a mini-lottery: You put down a small amount of money with the hopes of winning much much more, and then you lose. But it's a great movie game: It looks nice and everyone's standing up and it doesn't take long and it's immediately obvious whether the main character has won or lost and telekinetic space aliens can use their powers on it. **B**

Craps

The nice thing about craps is that they let you touch the dice. The same dice that the condo lothario next to you just breathed on, but it's a nice thought. The list of things to bet on is so long, and the names for each so obscure, that I'm always afraid that I'm going to accidentally bet on the croupier's age or something, but how can you not like a game where you can bet on "come"? **A**

Horse Racing

The best thing about horse racing is the names. The Boston Marathon would be much more interesting, in my opinion, if the contestants gave themselves names like "Her Majesty's Footstool" and "Son of Ziggurat." The other good things are the big mess of tickets left over afterward and the fact that the horses and jockeys wear matching outfits. **B–**

Video Poker

I can understand the appeal in gambling terms for people who want to feel as if they control their fate without actually doing so, but what I can't understand is the appeal of handheld electronic video poker where you can't actually win anything. I realize the importance of pretending everyone else doesn't exist at bus stops, but at least *People* magazine gives you something to talk about around the coffeemaker. **D**

Slots

There are a huge variety of slot machines, especially considering they all work the same way. Slot machines, for best effect, should have deceptively generous-sounding names. Good names include "Winner's Circle," "Lucky Duck," and "Rich Bastard." Bad names would be "Second Mortgage," "Car-Floor Change Scrounge," and "The Purpose of This Call Is to Collect a Debt." **C–**

GREEK GODS

Gaia

Ah, yes, Gaia, the warm, loving earth mother who made a sickle so that one of her sons could castrate another one of her sons, who also happened to be his brother and her husband. This, along with the fact that most of Gaia's offspring were monsters, hundred-handed giants and the like, makes hers a story more likely to go over well at a David Lynch film festival than at a solstice retreat/drum circle. **C–**

Zeus

Zeus became the head god by dint of not being eaten by his father. Consider that a sort of eighth habit of highly effective people: Very few of those in positions of power and authority were devoured at birth. Zeus released his previously swallowed siblings and defeated his father, became ruler of the sky and land, and in turn devoured his first wife, Metis, for fear of being overthrown by his own children. A lot of this goes on in Greek mythology; it's like those Looney Tunes in which Sylvester swallows Tweety Bird and Tweety goes on to have a long conversation with whomever else Sylvester had eaten that day. **C+**

Ares

I was hoping to blow the lid off the perennial representation of Ares as a bloodthirsty jerk of a god, but a little research shows that, nope, he's a jerk. And a bloodthirsty one at that. If you want Ares to get his due, you have to skip over to the Romans, who loved this guy. They called him Mars and talked about how noble it was to get offed in his name. But the Greeks, being more interested in olive oil and hypotenuses than world conquest, wanted little to do with him. Good for them. **D+**

Aphrodite

Aphrodite was the god of love, desire, and, if you watch *Xena*, peroxide. She arose from the sea after the severed genitals of Uranus were discarded there. I just want to point out that I'm not looking for the particularly gruesome bits from Greek mythology. You can't read two pages through a book of Greek myths without running into severed genitals, baby eating, vomit, sex with animals, liver extraction, and similar horrors. It's like Bulfinch meets Troma. Anyhow. Aphrodite had a magical girdle. Good for her. **B−**

Dionysus

I'm not going to go into how Dionysus was born. Suffice to say it fits right in with the other godly birth stories and involves Zeus's thigh. At any rate, Dionysus attracted a cult following of women who drank a lot and went into periodic fits of utter madness, which is pretty much what I'm trying to do with my Web page. It's too late for me to be raised by mountain nymphs as he was, but I do what I can with what I have. It was the feasts of Dionysus that inspired the early Greeks to invent theater, so you could say that in a round-about way Dionysus is responsible for the whole folderol surrounding *The Phantom Menace*. Good for him. **A**

DANCES

The Macarena

This was a Bobbit-level topic on the stand-up circuit for a while, so I'll keep it short. Invent a dance for people who can't deal with line dancing because of the whole simultaneous legs-arms thing and you'll be rich, or at least successful, or at least a major topic on the stand-up circuit. Heeeeey, lame! **D**

The Twist

See above. Unlike the Macarena, the Twist approaches the problem of coordination between the upper and lower body by making them do essentially the same thing over and over again. And, I might add, over and over and over again. I've seen women in Elvis movies work in a little hop at the lower point of the Twist cycle, but that's about it for working your own aesthetic sensibility into the dance. **C**

The Electric Slide

This is the only line dance I know, and I learned it back when they were called "dances." Actually, I learned it at a Dude Ranch where it was called the "Texas Freeze." Given that in Texas, "Texas" is an adjective meaning "intended to appeal to men with huge belt buckles," I shouldn't have been surprised. **B–**

The Bump

Man, there is nothing dumber looking than a missed Bump. You know when you're walking down the street talking to a friend who stopped to look at a Magritte poster two blocks ago? Tom Jones–level suavity compared to the feeling of snappily swinging your hips toward your dance partner and hitting him or her in the stomach. **C**

The Conga

I know that as someone who has danced the Electric Texas Freeze Slide at every wedding he's attended, I am in no position to criticize, but, uh, no. If I'm going to get involved in this sort of mob mentality I want to be smashing the state and/or fighting the power, not kicking my leg out to the side like a demure Rockette. And don't even get me started on the Bunny Hop. **D**

QUIZ:
PORN STAR OR
MY LITTLE PONY?

Porn Star	Pony	
☐	☐	Cherry Treats
☐	☐	Lucky Star
☐	☐	Love Melody
☐	☐	Daisy Sweet
☐	☐	Sunshine Blue
☐	☐	Honey Rose
☐	☐	Ruby Lips
☐	☐	Misty Rain
☐	☐	Green Eyes
☐	☐	Heart Throb
☐	☐	Chocolate Delight
☐	☐	Sweetie Pie

ANSWERS:

Cherry Treats:
 A white and red "Sweetberry Pony." A horse that
 smells like cherries. Huh.

Lucky Star:
 He appeared in "Pure Milk #2." Sequels are never as
 good as the original, are they?

Love Melody:
 A "Twice as Fancy" pony. That's pretty darn fancy.

Daisy Sweet:
  This pony smelled like perfume. How come they never
  made one that smelled like a horse?
Sunshine Blue:
  Starred with about half a dozen women with only one
  name in "Fresh Flesh."
Honey Rose:
  She was in "Lethal Squirt." I don't want to know what
  "Lethal Squirt" is.
Ruby Lips:
  This, incredibly enough, was a pony. Sometimes I
  wonder if the designers themselves weren't watching
  porn films . . .
Misty Rain:
  "Strap-On Sally," "Foot Fetish Fantasies #2," "Tracey
  at the Sex Derby," "The XXX Files." This woman has
  quite a resume.
Green Eyes:
  He was in "Hispanic Heatwave" with a guy named
  "Skelator." No, really.
Heart Throb:
  A "So-Soft" Pegasus Pony. I try to avoid buying toys
  with "Throb" in the name.
Chocolate Delight:
  A "Soda-Sippin' Pony." It came with a straw. I really
  don't understand this.
Sweetie Pie:
  I'm really disturbed to know that there even exists
  a video called "Breastman's American Butt Search,"
  much less that someone named "Sweetie Pie"
  appears in it.

Give yourself one point for each correct answer.
  0–4 points: It's not just that you don't know about
                 porn and ponies, it's that you actively
                 get them confused. Think about what
                 that indicates.

5–8 points: You scored approximately as well as a computer picking answers at random, but at least you have free will.

9–11 points: You clearly know something about My Little Pony toys or porn, or both. Hopefully not both.

12 points: Congratulations! You're an expert on the equine and the supine!

BATH TOYS

Rubber Ducks

Rubber bath ducks that don't squeak are just sad. They inspire in me the sort of sympathy I normally reserve for three-legged dogs and little girls who are forced to wear miniature versions of their mother's outfits. What else does a rubber duck have to offer? Buoyancy and a cheerful expression, but what use is that in a quackless world? **B**

Tugboats

I don't get it. The purpose of tugboats is to shove around larger, less maneuverable seacraft, so why provide a tugboat bath toy and not an oil tanker or a garbage barge? If this doesn't bug tugboat operators, I've tragically overestimated them yet again. **C**

Soap

Plain old regular soap isn't that exciting, but luckily the many corporations with a financial interest in keeping our waterlogged youngsters amused have come up with several variations, including soap with which you can paint your face, soap with which you can draw on the tile, and soap that pours like ectoplasm out of your favorite marketable cartoon characters. If there's no edible soap, it's only because that would be a really really bad idea. **C+**

Squirty Fish

Like drums and toy swords, these are toys that parents know can only lead to aggravation. There are so many ways to get water out of the tub and onto the grout that there hardly need to be playthings that are specifically designed for that purpose. You may as well give the kids a pump siphon and go hit the towel closet. **C–**

Bubbles

Bubble bath may not technically come under the category of toys, but tell that to anyone who's played Voltron Conquers Bubble Mountain. Bubbles can be used as landscaping, jewelry, sculpting material, and a low-grade science experiment, all within the same bath. **A**

WAYS TO SEND MAIL

Postcards

Lately, the United States Postal Service has taken to putting big sticky bar codes at the bottom of postcards, often obscuring important information, like why Gary decided not to try the swordfish. Why in the name of all that is properly stamped is a public institution consistently interfering with the ability of mail to convey information? Literacy is low enough in this country without effectively requiring all postcards to have fewer than ten words on them. **C–**

E-mail

In principle, e-mail is the most excellent use of computers since the first moon shot, but in practice a combination of spam, misinformation, and lame humor mailings have made it similar to trying to have a conversation in a whorehouse while scam artists tell you a hundred ways to annoy the pizza guy while dying of Aspartame poisoning. It makes me long for the days when "mail" meant fifty-page letters ending with "May Providence cast His gentle Beneficence upon you as I remain your humble Servant in times of both Peace and Strife with Deepest and most Sincere Regards, Doctor Lord Reverend Baron Thyme-Parsely Esq." **C+**

Voice Mail

The whole issue of voice mail and answering machine etiquette is quite thorny. I have friends, for instance, who have answering machines that have a long, annoying dial tone whenever anyone hangs up, which they hate, so I have a habit of waiting for the beep, saying "Courtesy message, bye" and hanging up. Okay for answering machines but it's perplexing to get on voice mail. Even worse on voice mail are people who say "Hello? Hello? Pick up if you're there. Pick up!" to the soulless machine recording their voices. And then there's that note of disappointment in the voices of those who wanted to get your machine and now have to pretend they care how your day is going. **B−**

Faxes

Faxes are low resolution and often impossible to read, but at least they don't usually require icky-feeling paper rolls anymore. And I prefer them at least to e-mail attachments, which are always in Microsoft Word and make me feel like I should just pour my life's blood into a freezer bag and mail it to Bill Gates and get it over with. **C**

Actual Letters

I like writing letters, but at the same time they increasingly make me feel like I'm being a willful anachronism, like my peers who wear capes and poet shirts because they think it makes them look like Romantic Era dreamboats and not at all like big geeks. I'm wasting paper, spending money, and making friends wait a week because I think ink looks pretty. Ah, well, hand me the cape. **A**

PARTY GAMES

I Never

This is the game where one person points out one activity—inevitably sexual—that he or she has never done, and those who have done that very thing have to take a drink. It's a typical attempt to introduce sex into the conversation and alcohol into the bloodstream at the same time, but isn't that what parties are all about? I liked this game a lot until in a moment of thoughtlessness I mistakenly and falsely admitted to a sexual encounter with a roving troupe of street performers in the United Arab Emirates. **B+**

Charades

This is what happens when you don't drink. You end up making antler motions with your hands in front of a group of adults because you picked "Benito Mussolini." Yeah, charades can be turned into a drinking game, but anything can be turned into a drinking game, even AA-meeting bingo. **C–**

Truth or Dare

I swore off this one early. Not because of the truth part—I've admitted more embarrassing moments from my past than most people would think to ask, some in this very book—but because those dares get pretty freaky pretty quickly. Get a bunch of kids in early adolescence giving each other dares, and pretty soon you're going to have broken at least one commandment from every major religion, and several local statutes besides. **D**

Quarters

I'm not big on manual dexterity, especially while drinking, as many shirt-front Tia Maria stains can attest. Bouncing change into my drink seems like an insult to both beer and currency, and the statistical likelihood that any given quarter has passed through at least one porn-booth slot makes the whole thing unappealing in the extreme. **C–**

That Game Where You Pass Each Other Oranges Using Your Necks

I'm wary of pastimes that are transparent attempts to make people touch each other a bunch: this game, Twister, "I Bet You Could Use a Massage," that whole freaky Lambada fad, and so forth. I'm not against the touching, goodness heavens no. It's just the pretending. They're the party equivalent of "Whoops! I didn't know you were taking a bath in here." Let us grow up. **C–**

CARTOON ARCHENEMIES

Cats and Mice

Kind of overdone, but for good reason. Nobody doubts the validity of the rivalry, the mouse gets the sympathy vote, and when you're out of ideas, there are always walls to run into. I'm not sure where they got the idea that dogs are on the side of the mice, though. I understand the value of coalition building, but all the dogs I've ever met consider mice to be furry little Snausages. **A**

Roadrunners and Coyotes

Do actual coyotes eat actual roadrunners? I was under the impression that they were more into vole-based cuisine. But I'm fairly sure that coyotes don't own mail-order catalogs, either, so I'll just sit back and enjoy the head-flattening. **A**

Ducks and Mice

The point at which Looney Tunes lost their amoral compass is clear; when they decided to make Daffy Duck go up against Speedy Gonzales. Come again? I can't even remember why a duck was after a mouse in the first place. It involved either cheese or immigration policies. **D–**

Wolves and Redheads

God bless Tex Avery. Without his wisdom, how would we know that wolves were into zoot suits and henna? As a child, I was never quite sure what the wolves wanted with the redheads, although I was convinced that they wanted it very badly. I don't think this was out of any cluelessness on my part, but rather an instinctive understanding that the psychosexual implications of devouring/fornicating were something I didn't want to consider before I was old enough to drink. **A**

Hunters and Woodland Creatures

Mad props or whatever to Chuck Jones, the patron saint of animals with gunpowder-blackened faces. Many people point to "What's Opera, Doc?" as the masterwork of Merrie Melodies, but for my money (okay, my attention during commercial breaks) you can't do better than the "rabbit season/duck season" shorts. "Ah! Pronoun trouble!" is perhaps the funniest line from anything ever. **A**

EXERCISE EQUIPMENT

Stair Steppers

I love that the less we actually have to move to get around in this society, the more villainous our exercise gadgets become. Having nearly eliminated the need to climb flights of stairs, we then turn around and force ourselves to not only climb stairs, but to climb *endless* stairs. We don't even get a nice view at the top, because there's *no top*. It's the sort of thing Dante Alighieri would have come up with if he thought about abs more. **C**

Treadmill

Having blasted the idea of infinite stairs, I now have to admit that I like the idea of infinite walkways. This is for two reasons. First, if I just step outside and start strolling, I end up inhaling cubic liters of SUV flatulence. Secondly, I don't like the sun. It's hot and it makes my neck hurt after maybe a half hour. **B**

Weight Machines

Call it lack of important social training in junior high, call it an instinctive wariness, but I don't like asking random sweaty muscled people to help keep a metal bar from crushing my neck. So when in the mood to make large pieces of metal move a few inches, I'm much happier with weight training machines than with free weights. Plus, they're isometric, which is a Greek word meaning nothing of interest. **B–**

Ab-Building Sliding Machines

It's a proven scientific fact that I hate sit-ups. They're like being punched in the stomach, only spread out over several minutes and you get to keep your lunch money. And nothing improves this. No amount of footage of living Rodin sculptures pretending they got that way by scooting back and forth on a piece of plastic is going to convince me otherwise. Actual smelting would be a less painful way of getting abs of whatever alloy you prefer. **D**

Rowing Machines

Well, I dunno. At least you get to sit down. But I always feel like I'm in a wacky comedy in which the wacky star doesn't realize his canoe isn't in the water and this leads to a wacky double take. As alluring as I find the alliteration in the phrase "wacky workout," it's not a personal goal. **D+**

EPOCHS

Stone Age

I think people from the late Stone Age would be offended by the label. "Stone? Motherfucker, this is pottery, okay? I spent the better part of a moon-goes-away gathering mud out of the riverbank, shaping it into the attractive urn you see before you, and painting horn beasts on it, so don't give me any of that 'stone' crap. And this is carefully chipped flint. I'll take a flint-tipped spear and you take a rock and we'll see who gets sent into the arms of our wide-hipped goddess first, all right?" **C+**

Bronze Age

The names of the various epochs aren't strictly defined, and many people like to continue the materials-based nomen-clature, leading from the Bronze Age through the Iron Age, the Steel Age, and the very brief Bakelite Age in the fifties up to the current era, which I believe is the Low-Fat Salad Dressing Age. Anyhow. The Bronze Age is good because the helmets had fuzzy brushes on top. **C+**

Space Age

The term "Space Age" has fallen out of favor in the past couple of decades, presumably because while it seemed for a while that we might conquer the universe, our current space program is limited to inventing new ways to transmit television shows and throwing billion-dollar spitballs at Mars. *Captain Rocket Repairs a GPS Satellite* isn't the sort of book that keeps youngsters up till all hours. **C–**

Industrial Age

Roughly defined as "after factories were invented but before they were all moved to Malaysia," the Industrial Age ushered in many modern ills, including widespread pollution, depletion of natural resources, and smug books with marginally effective feel-good methods of reducing pollution and the depletion of natural resources. The main advantage is that it makes possible those little *Sesame Street* vignettes where they show you how milk is bottled or whatnot. I loved those. **D**

Information Age

Love the age, but not the name. It makes it sound as if information was discovered in the late eighties, when the feasibility of Antarctic expeditions finally made it possible to exploit the vast information deposits just under the surface. An early mining company brought millions of barrels of personal home pages back to the United States, but the industry didn't really take off until the discovery of what is now called the "Porn Chasm." Actually, that would have been cool. **B+**

Biotechnology Age

Historian gun-jumpers are in a rush to figure out what the next age will be, and the Biotechnology Age is one of the front-runners. In the Age of Biotechnology, we will have not machines but actual organisms doing our dirty work, from devouring radioactive waste to washing our cars with their long trunks. Just like on *The Flintstones*, the Modern Biotechnology Age Family. **D**

QUIZ:
ARE YOU COMIC RELIEF?

Yes No

☐ ☐ 1. After a dangerous adventure is over, have you ever found yourself wrapped up completely in recording tape as your friends look on and laugh?

☐ ☐ 2. Do you have a speech impediment?

☐ ☐ 3. Are your eyes significantly larger than those of your friends?

☐ ☐ 4. Have you ever, under any circumstances, leapt into someone's arms in fright?

☐ ☐ 5. If you and your friends have all been given advanced magical or technological devices, are you stuck with the one that hardly ever works?

☐ ☐ 6. Is your hat too big?

☐ ☐ 7. Are you the only unarmed person within forty meters?

☐ ☐ 8. When your show or movie is made into a fast-food kids' meal, are you the alternative "toddler-safe" toy?

☐ ☐ 9. Does most Internet fan fiction about you address your grisly and prolonged death?

☐ ☐ 10. Are you the only member of your group with a sense of self-preservation and/or math skills?

SCORING: Give yourself one point for each "yes."

0 points:	You are not comic relief.
1–3 points:	You are probably not comic relief, but you may become so in subsequent sequels and/or seasons if the writers run out of ideas.
4–6 points:	To check whether you are comic relief, comment out loud that "at least it's not raining." If it immediately begins to rain, you're it.
7–10 points:	You are comic relief. You're going to spend the rest of your life leaning up against big red levers, mistaking your friends for the villain, and uttering the phrase "That's what I'm afraid of!" But at least it'll be a long life, unless Frank Miller gets script duties.

ALIEN INVADERS

E.T.

Okay, more of a tourist than an invader, but it's tough to tell the difference sometimes. You notice there's not a lot of *E.T.* nostalgia out there, compared to, say, *Star Wars*. I think this is because of the hanky factor. Looking back on the first time you saw *Star Wars*, you think "Robots! Starfighters! I was on the edge of my seat!" Looking back on *E.T.*, you think "I cried like a preschooler over the death of a walking sausage." **C–**

Grays

The problem with these guys is that as alien invaders go, they seem to lack a master plan. You'd think forty years of abductions would provide them with all the biological data they need. My suspicion is that they're not actually softening us up for eventual tyrannical domination, as one might hope, but rather just filling some sort of interplanetary government job in the Bureau of Abduction and Unpleasant Probing, Sweater-Wearing Primate Division. **C**

Audrey II

If flesh-eating alien invaders have traditionally suffered from one drawback, it's that they didn't sing R&B music. Thankfully, this was remedied when they made *Little Shop of Horrors* into a musical. Now, if they just take my advice and make a movie about a terpsichorean vampire called *Dark Lord of the Dance*. **B+**

Those Aliens from *Independence Day*

I have to say, I'm torn on these guys. On one hand, any species that can be taken out with one punch by a rapper-cum-sitcom-star has some serious lack going on, but on the other hand, I'm damn impressed with the Dead Brent Spiner Hand Puppet Trick. I really think they should take that one on the road. A gooey alien with a talking Brent Spiner corpse is about the only thing that could get me to watch *Live at the Improv*. **B–**

Cylons

They eventually invaded, in the TV movie *Galactica 1980*, which is the name of my favorite roller disco. You gotta love these guys, for various and sundry reasons. First, there's the throbbing robot eye, which set a standard for cheesy TV sci-fi effects and influenced, um, *Knight Rider*. Second, the head Cylon was named Imperious Leader. Now that's a title. Third, they talk with the same computer-generated monotone that nearly destroyed the world in *WarGames*. **B+**

The Aliens from *War of the Worlds*

They came. They blew things up. They were destroyed by microbes. More important, they weren't destroyed by a computer virus or time travel. A model hostile alien force. If that isn't enough to convince you, note that the movie was recorded in "Western Electric Multi-Track Magnetic Stereophonic Sound," and the poster slogan called the film a "mighty panorama of Earth-shaking fury as an army from Mars invades." Any invaders that can inspire that many adjectives get my vote. **A**

WORD PROBLEMS

Trains Approaching Each Other

When trains are eventually made obsolete by antigrav subterranean parcel movers, it's going to ruin a lot of word
problems, not to mention prison songs ("When I feel that
antigrav subterranean parcel mover rumbling/I hang my
head and cry/Unless it's just the washing machine").
They'll just be replaced with antigrav subterranean parcel
mover problems, but for some reason there will be no
abbreviation for "antigrav subterranean parcel movers," so
at least there'll be fewer of them per page. **B–**

Apples

I am perplexed by the cultural obsession with apples as the
only fruit worth mentioning. Even oranges rarely seem to
get any publicity outside of the fact that one shouldn't compare them to apples. Would it kill us to add and subtract
mangoes or refer to the durians of our individual and col-
lective eyes? **C**

Change

Money is a great motivator. People realize this. Making
change is a great way to get the small fry to realize that yes,
they're going to have to do this math stuff all their lives
unless they're going to trust that guy at the U-Haul with the
torn name tag that reads "Stev" to do right by them. **B+**

Canoes

The problem with elementary school education is that it lies. Getting simple concepts across often requires one to omit the subtleties, so we get to eighth grade thinking that hydrogen molecules look like abstracted nipples, that Pluto is always the furthest planet from the sun, and that rivers drive canoes downstream at a constant and predictable rate. It's a sad state of affairs, but try telling that to Mrs. Grebach of Live Oak Elementary. **D+**

Ages

Actual mathematical questions involving age in the real world are usually very simple, like "Was your girlfriend even born when you finished law school?" and "Is there any chance that I'll still be alive when Kate Bush gets around to releasing another album?" This is as opposed to age questions in math tests that ask you to figure out how many years old Roberto will be when he's twice as old as Li if Li is one-third Roberto's age and six years younger than Roberto is now. These questions are useless once you leave school, unless you're the sort of person who is trying to solve the above problem right now. **C–**

BUMPER STICKER SLOGANS

"My Child Has Received Some Sort of Honor from His or Her Educational Institution"

These are about as impressive as a Certificate of Participation, but I realize that they're not for my edification, any more than crayon drawings are attached to refrigerators so that I can indulge my aesthetic soul. These things are on bumpers from sea to underachieving sea because if your child receives one—and your child will—and you don't put it on your car, that child will become a criminal and blame you as he or she is dragged wild-eyed into the courthouse. **C–**

"Presidential Candidate/Running Mate Election Year"

Perhaps I'm politically spineless, but I've never had such a strong level of support for a candidate that I've been willing to go on telling people to vote for him several years after his overwhelming, humiliating defeat. Some people are, however, until the next election adds another sticker to the visibly growing stack of grassroots support. **C**

"99.9 FM 'The Station' "

It's interesting that people advertise radio stations on their bumpers for free, sometimes even paying for the privilege. It's interesting that bumper stickers are approximately the same aspect ratio as a banner ad on the Web. It's interesting that the print ends up being about the same size proportionally. It's interesting that nobody seemed to notice this before the Web ad business dried up like a hog waller in a comet strike. **B–**

"My Other Car Is a Humorous Comment"

There's a trend in American humor for parody to outgrow and outlive the material being mocked. The short-lived spate of "Baby on Board" stickers of the eighties turned into a longer-lived procession of supposedly clever variations thereon. Similarly, even the proudest Porsche or Saab owner would have a hard time finding a sticker assuring unconcerned onlookers that they have a better (or similar) car at home, but those whose other cars are bicycles, up on blocks, or pieces of shit have a literal embarrassment of choices. **D+**

Various Innocuous Antidrug Slogans

I'm not convinced of the efficacy of public service announcements—having received more pseudo-hip instructions to stay off drugs, follow the rules, and respect Nancy Reagan than hot meals during my childhood—but public service announcements attached to moving vehicles strike me as especially unlikely to set an otherwise wayward youth on the straight and narrow. I'm not saying that nobody ever gave up drugs because they saw a catchy acronym attached to an SUV, but that's only because the whole idea is so ludicrous I shouldn't *have* to say it. **D**

REFERENCE BOOKS

Dictionaries

While I don't always agree with dictionaries on the subjects of whether words actually exist and, if they do, whether you can add "-tabulous" to the end of them, and I think they're quoted too often by people who write letters to the editor but who can't think of a good lead-in, I have to say I love them. From providing information in my youth on exactly what a "hymen" is to helping me remember what the word "irony" means so that I can give Alanis a hard time about not knowing the same, dictionaries have comforted and educated me since I moved up to the ones where not every word is illustrated. **A**

Atlases

The great thing about atlases is that they go out of date so quickly. Each one is like a little time capsule, the geopolitical equivalent of your high school yearbook. "Remember when everyone was trying to get East Germany and West Germany to get together, but they were all like 'no way'? God, we were such dorks then!" **A–**

Thesauruses

Thesauruses are a constant source of disappointment for me, because as often as not it turns out that when I can't think of a word, it's because it hasn't been invented. It's kind of a bummer to find out that there isn't actually a word that kind of means "unclean" but implies a careful sort of unclean, like someone who chooses their filth carefully for aesthetic, but not offensive, effect. No, "dowdy" isn't it. **B**

AP Style Guide

I ♥ the AP style guide. I love the idea that there are several someones out there who look at each new world-changing invention or development and ask themselves what usage problems it's going to present. "Jesus has returned to the earth and is doing battle with the armies of Satan! Is it 'the stars are fallen from their spheres' or 'the stars *have* fallen from their spheres'?" **A**

Who's Who

The various Who's Who (and shouldn't that be "Who's Whom"?) books seem too quaint to me, like leather chairs next to elegant little tables with brandy snifters on them in rooms with dead animal heads on the walls where old men referred to by their former military ranks take long naps. Between mass murderers and software tyrants, these days the important question isn't "Who's who?" but rather "Who isn't who yet but will be in three years and how are they going to fuck up my life this time?" **D**

RODEO EVENTS

Bull Riding

Bull riding is the ultimate mix of hubris and humility. Here are these denim-clad good old boys strapping themselves to the back of a huge, horned animal with ropes squeezing its scrotum, and they're wearing *hats*. That's hubris. The humility part is that they're only expected to stay atop the things for eight seconds. **B+**

Calf Roping

Nothing quite as macho as running down a bleating baby cow and tying it up, is there? At least compared to the "duckling lob." My favorite part is that they raise their arms with an almost majestic finality when they're done, as if to say "Voila! The calf is trussed, as the legends foretold!" **C–**

Bronc Busting

Very similar to the bull thing, but there's more to say: I like how you get more points the more cantankerous your animal is. It must be interesting to be really good at bronc riding and hoping to get the one that most wants to stomp you into a cowpoke-shaped stain. **B**

Barrel Riding

I have no doubt that this requires incredible reflexes and an almost primal empathic link with your animal, but I wish it weren't just running around in circles. It's like watching the world's greatest athletes compete to see who can stand up and sit down the most times in two minutes. **D**

Sheep Riding

As with nearly every organized sport outside of oil wrestling, rodeo has a Little League. When the leaguers are very little, I am told they participate in sheep riding, a competition that is precisely what you'd expect. Small children cling to running sheep. I must witness this. It sounds inexpressibly wonderful. **B**

COFFEE SHOP DRINKS

Espresso

Espresso has always struck me as the intellectual's equivalent of movie cowboys ordering rye whiskey in a dirty shot glass. It has the same connotation of ritualistic self-abuse in a community setting, only with more elaborate preparation. I back this up with the observation that all the praise I hear for espresso is for its potency rather than for its flavor. **B**

Con Panna

Con panna is Euro-speak for "I'd like Redi-Whip on that, please." Once in a *luna azzurra*, you find a shop that makes a dense, bitter whipped cream that goes well with the espresso, but by and large you get crappy fluffy whipped cream, leading to a sort of disconcerting Swiss-Miss-goes-domme effect. **C–**

Iced Mocha

Mochae of any sort are lovely, but iced mocha on a hot day makes me happy to be alive, in the literal sense that it forcibly alters my brain chemistry. I've had some that were artistically choreographed into existence, and some that were slapped together mechanistically, but like pizza and movies with "bikini" in the title, even when they're bad, they're good. **A+**

Americano

Possibly the greatest slur against American culture since—well, all the other really memorable slurs against American culture have come from Americans, so it's hard to compare. In an apparent retaliatory strike against General Foods "International" Coffees, continentals have decided to water down their espresso and blame us. Suffice to say the failings of espresso are emphasized and the admirable qualities minimized in this malconceived concoction. **D**

Chai

One of the great things about the West Coast is that we appropriate the food of other cultures first. Californians were enjoying pesto and sushi while Midwesterners were still getting used to the concept of salad bars. Chai, spicy East Indian tea mixed with milk, was until recently very difficult to track down in the United States outside of certain cities on the California coast, but it has since become a staple of the caffeine-inhaling scene. This is all very self-aggrandizing, I know, but I have to make myself feel better about the fact that most restaurants in California wouldn't know a rare steak if it bled on them. **B+**

AESOP'S FABLES

The Fox and the Grapes

I'm not sure what the point is here. The moral is "It is easy to despise what you cannot get," but from experience I can tell you it's easy to despise what you do get, as well, especially in terms of cable channels. I was going to be skeptical of the idea of a fox eating grapes in the first place, but apparently they're omnivores, so that checks out. Still, it would have been slightly more reasonable to have the fox chasing after a vole or something, and then the English language would contain the phrase "Oh, that's just sour voles." **C–**

The Tortoise and the Hare

"Slow but steady wins the race." This is untrue. Generally speaking, slow but steady loses the race rather humiliatingly. Slow but steady wins the pie-eating contest. The story is amusing enough, but the moral should be changed to "Slow but steady wins the race if all the other participants are narcoleptics," or alternatively, "Don't be a moron." **D**

The Mice and the Weasels

You probably don't know this one. In brief, a bunch of mice appoint mouse generals in their war with the weasels. The mouse generals wear elaborate hats and get eaten because in the inevitable retreat, they can't fit back in the mouse holes. In spite of what Aesop would have you believe, this has absolutely no application to life in general, but I still like it because it's about weasels. **B–**

The North Wind and the Sun

This is a little obscure, but you've probably heard it. The North Wind and the Sun have a little contest to see who can make a random passerby get naked, which is remarkably similar to a game I played in college. The North Wind can't blow the guy's clothes off, but the Sun persuades him to take his clothes off by buying him beers and telling him he looks like Julia Roberts. Or something like that. **C**

The Wolf in Sheep's Clothing

Hey, what a handy little fable. At long last we have a useful lesson—don't judge by appearances—and an interesting little story with a violent ending and everything. Not that it's easy to picture a wolf being at all convincing with a sheepskin thrown over its shoulders, but it's also hard to imagine George Clooney as an avenging crime fighter, so every era has its problems. **A**

QUIZ:
ARE WE THERE YET?

1. Are we there yet?
   - ☐ No.
   - ☐ Almost.
2. Are we there yet?
   - ☐ We've still got a ways to go.
   - ☐ I'll let you know when we get there.
3. Are we there yet?
   - ☐ Pipe down and play your Game Boy.
   - ☐ Hey, look! Sheep!
4. Are we there yet?
   - ☐ Stop asking or I'm going to turn this car around right now!
   - ☐ I told you, I'll let you know when we get there.
5. Are we there yet?
   - ☐ God dammit, don't make me reach back there and smack you!
   - ☐ God dammit, don't make me pull the car over and smack you!

SCORING: Give yourself one point if we are there.
  0 points: We are not there yet.
  1 point: We are there.

SPEED RACER CHARACTERS

Speed Racer

What is it that makes Speed so great? Is it his injection-molded hair? His Swedish-porn-star scarf? The fact that his eyelashes are larger than most North American songbirds? He looks like a woodland creature, if woodland creatures bought all their clothes from Fingerhut catalogs and had poorly synchronized speech. He's the very paragon of glistening nobility and he has a cool car. He's so dreamy. **A+**

Trixie

If Barbie is a poor physical role model for young girls, Trixie is a poor physical role model for yearling gazelles. I don't know if her coffee-stirrer legs and arms were designed to conserve valuable ink, or if the head animator had a thing for coat racks, or what, but nonetheless she's still not as pretty as Speed. Is she Speed's girlfriend? Their relationship seems based not so much on romance as on her making little worried noises all the time. Soul mate or designated fretter? **C**

The Narrator

The narrative voice isn't as active in the *Racer* oeuvre as it is in, say, the *Super Friends*, but when it does show up, it's always awful. A sampling: "Meanwhile, in a secret hotel room, the secret head of the Alpha Team, Mr. Wiley, is having a secret meeting." Frankly, if it's that secret, I'm surprised anyone showed up. The only real purpose the narrator serves is to say "And here are some bad guys," which isn't really necessary, because *Speed Racer* bad guys all look distinctively like 1960s joke cocktail napkin characters. **D**

Racer X

It's not often you find masked riders at major non-wrestling sporting events, which is a shame because they inevitably lend a jaunty air to the proceedings. At any rate, Racer X—secretly Speed's prodigal brother, Rex—is living proof of the saying "Any crash you can walk away from, disown your father, leave home, return years later as a masked mystery figure, and nearly accidentally kill your brother in an impromptu nighttime car race is a good one." Profound. **B+**

Pops Racer

Pops exemplifies Lamarck's Theory of Evolution by Means of Last Name. Each generation of Racers has gotten better and better at racing; simulations predict that Speed's great-great-grandchild will be able to break the world land speed record in a Geo Metro. If Pops's last name were Typist or Pusher, it would have been a very different, although probably still inexplicably entertaining, cartoon. This also explains why you see so few people with the last names of Loser, Failure, or High Insurance Risk. **C+**

Spritle and Chim-Chim

Really, really disturbing. If they didn't wear the same outfits, or even if the outfits didn't include those Spanky-by-way-of-Dr.-Seuss skullcaps, I could probably take it. I recognize how essential their loathsome shenanigans are to the *Speed Racer* look and feel, but I'm hoping Spritle's hard at work suppressing memories, because otherwise he's going to have a lot of trouble forming functional relationships later on in life. "Could you grunt like a monkey, baby? Yeah. Now do a backflip. Now try to steal my candy. Oh yeah, baby." **C**

NATIONAL SPORTS

Buzkashi

You know, as do all intelligent people, that Afghanistan has the only national sport to require a decapitated goat carcass. I'd be inclined to wonder why the decapitated part is so important, but you know, it's a sport. Baseball has four bases, football requires ten yards for a first down, and in buzkashi the goat has to be headless. It's just the way things are. **C–**

Cricket

I don't want to start any stupid transatlantic arguments, but I think it's worth noting that British sportswriters have criticized baseball for being too fast and rowdy compared to cricket. While I enjoy baseball, I have never once wished it were slower. That's like wishing that Three Musketeers bars were less nutritious. I do, however, like the phrase "sticky wicket," which I'm pretty sure is from either cricket or Ewok porn. **C+**

Sumo

There's something pleasant about a sport where the objective is clear from the get-go, and there's nothing much clearer than "Shove the other guy harder than he shoves you," especially in a country as crowded as Japan. Americans tend to think of sumo as "the fat-guy sport," which is kind of ironic considering that most of the world thinks of the United States as "the fat-guy country." **B**

Football

By "football," I of course mean "soccer," the national sport of the country of, jeez, just about everywhere. I'm not sure why one would bother to name the single most popular sport in the world as one's "national" sport. It's like naming water your national drink. Nobody's going to say "Uruguay . . . that's the place that's really into soccer, right?" **C**

Bullfighting

To be fair, I think this should just be a bull and a guy. Each gets to use what God gave him (i.e., horns and the sense not to do this in the first place, respectively) and we can see who wins. I think the guys should still wear the flashy outfits with the "sad Mickey Mouse" hats, and they should still get to keep their ears if they win. "Ears awarded" is a great sports stat. **D+**

BATMAN'S SIDEKICKS

Robin

I never liked Robin. I never understood Robin. I'm told that Robin was invented to give kids someone to identify with, but I never wanted to be a spindly teenager with elf slippers and a ornothological code name; I wanted to be Batman! The only good things about Robin are that he gave Batman someone to talk to when working out the Riddler's stupid clues and he's someone to make your younger sibling be when playing superheroes. **D+**

Batwoman

This one is different from Batgirl. Batwoman came along in the fifties and she had—get this—a *utility purse*, from which she pulled weaponry like a *compact* with a *mirror* and an *expanding hair net*. Comic books have never been known for their Faludi-approved portrayals of women, but the idea of a makeup-powered crime fighter makes Wonder Woman and her Amazon hot pants look like *A Room of One's Own* by comparison. **D+**

Batgirl

What can I say, I have a thing for redheads in cowls. It's a shame Ann-Margret never got the role. Anyhow, Batgirl fills out the "female version" niche of the standard superhero chess set quite adequately. The important and unnerving thing to note here is that someone has put together a Web page of all the ways Batgirl has been tied up and restrained in her long and illustrious career as a spandex-clad hostage. Weird. Eerie. Contains the phrase "dunked in frozen caviar." **B**

Ace, the Bat-Hound

Next step on the sidekick express is the inevitable animal sidekick. He didn't appear in many issues, thank Ditko. I could explain the whole origin thing, but you know what? It's dumb. Ace was a dog with a secret identity. He didn't have any superpower or, as far as I know, technologically advanced chew toys. He was a dog in a mask. Let's move on. **C–**

Bat-Mite

Apparently once comic book writers are completely and utterly out of useful ideas, they introduce deformed annoying versions of their main character. Superman gets you Bizarro, Captain Marvel gets you Uncle Marvel (don't ask), and Batman gets you Bat-Mite, an imp from one of the many dimensions located inside some writer's ass who exists to terrorize Batman because of hero-worship. Bat-Mite's saving grace is that he annoys Batman as much as he annoys the reader. His main failing is that he never receives a savage beating from one of Batman's angrier incarnations. **D+**

STAR TREK ALIEN MAKEUP

Vulcan Ears

Spock ears may be the driving force behind the *Trek* phenomenon. Roddenberry apparently tapped into one of the strongest symbols in the Universal Geek Unconscious. Somewhere in the back of the mind of every D&D-playing junior high schooler is the equation "pointy ears = cool." Elves, Vulcans, Yoda, six-breasted Cat Women—wherever you find dweeby wish fulfillment, you find pointy ears. **B–**

Bajoran Nose Ridges

Man, they weren't even trying with this one. I don't know if they were running out of latex or what, but boldly going where people look like they're about to go cross-eyed is not my idea of majestic space opera. Coming soon—aliens with extra-deep upper lip dents. **D**

Klingon Forehead Ridges

I've heard rumors that the Klingon term for forehead ridges is "flavor curls," but I doubt that we're getting confirmation on that one anytime soon. I'm sure the Klingons took home the Most Improved Makeup award at the Implausible Aliens Convention, but they never did explain how they got to their present impressive state from the original series, where on the special effects scale they rated slightly below "Endora turns Darren into a mule." **B+**

Andorian Antennae

Yeah, I realize even acknowledging the existence of Andorian antennae pegs me as Signori Molti di Geekland, but that's the price you pay for thoroughness. To my credit, I don't know what purpose the antennae supposedly serve, but I imagine they had something to do with natural selection, early in the Andorians' evolution, for life-forms that looked completely fakey. This also accounts for the blue skin and the Caesar-cum-Sno-Balls hairdo. **C–**

Cardassian Neck Cables

There's something really stylish about the Cardassians, with their suspension-bridge necks and *Trainspotting*-meets-Transylvania sunken eyes, the entire look conspiring to say "I was assembled from an Erector Set and I may destroy you at any moment." Overall, I never really dug the Cardassians—the Borg could have assimilated their asses faster than you can say "Mr. Tambourine Man"—but the look was there. **B**

Ferengi Teeth

I know the ears and foreheads are supposed to be the attraction here—how novel for a *Star Trek* alien—but I'm always fascinated by the Ferengis' teeth. All other races in the galaxy seem to have discovered corrective orthodontia and no-copayment dental plans; the Ferengi alone dare to keep their teeth looking like Stonehenge on mescaline. Considering that even the warrior-class Klingons must be flossing, this is an admirable resistance to interspecies peer pressure. **B**

WIZARD OF OZ CHARACTERS

The Scarecrow

He may have lacked a brain, but he obviously had some sort of rudimentary nervous system, probably straw based. I do wonder how an ordinary scarecrow became an agricultural Frosty the Snowman. Presumably he was unique; if Munchkin scarecrows were universally inclined to run off on vision quests, I imagine Munchkin farmers would have just switched to buckshot. Maybe it's covered in one of the four hundred Oz books I haven't read, *Slave Girls of Oz* or something. **C+**

The Tin Woodman

Who could help but have empathy with this rusting rustic? A less kind metallic lumberjack would have realized that he had an axe, Dorothy had a heart, put two and two together, and invented the slasher flick forty years early. On one hand, that would have pretty much ruined the heartwarmingness of the movie. On the other hand, it would have generated sequels like *Tin Woodman IX: Die, Glinda, Die.* **B+**

Dorothy

Dorothy sure had a way of befriending freaks, didn't she? I'm surprised she didn't end up adding a kleptomaniac bronze emu to her little enchanted convoy. And not once did she point out to her companions that their lack of emotional stability and/or body parts was not, technically speaking, her problem. She just helped and gave and sympathized and offed witches when told to. Maybe she should have asked the Wizard for a spine. **C**

The Cowardly Lion

Sure, it's nice for the lion that he got some emerald therapy from the wiz, but what about the antelope of Oz? Do you think Dorothy would have helped out a cowardly antelope? Unlikely. Antelope are *supposed* to be cowardly, or at least nervous, but you show the little Kansan a cowardly *lion*—the one lion no antelope need fear—and she falls all over her gingham hemline to turn him into a murderous carnivore. And yes, I know that female lions do all the hunting. I'm trying to make a *point* here. **C–**

The Wicked Witch of the West

If water were the one thing that could kill me, I certainly wouldn't go leaving big buckets of it lying around my evil castle. That's like a normal person having a sulfuric acid hot tub in the backyard. And yet the WWW seemed so surprised. "Oh, gosh, I'm dying here. I don't suppose there's any way I could have forseen this? No, because I'm dumb." **D**

THE SEVEN DWARVES

Grumpy

There seems to be a rule that every group of lovable anthropoids has to have a troubled brooder. *Sesame Street* has Oscar, Winnie-the-Pooh has Eeyore, the Smurfs—I apologize for knowing this—have Grouchy, and the Seven Dwarves have Grumpy. I suppose, if you get right down to it, this trend was started by the Apostles. It's hard to imagine Grumpy leading the Pharisees to Snow White for thirty pieces of silver, then hanging himself at a crossroads, but it's worth the effort. **C**

Doc

Poor Doc, doomed forever to be a noun dwarf among adjective dwarves. I wonder how he got the name. Is it just that he's the smartest one (not that any of them come across as Rhodes scholars) or does he have some sort of fantasy medical degree? Either way, it didn't help him when Snow White literally bit the big one. If only he had read "Osculatory Revivification in Cases of Enchanted Narcolepsy" in the prestigious *Journal of Fruit-Borne Curses.* **C+**

Happy

Happy may have been the most forgettable dwarf of the bunch. I can't even conjure up his face in my mind, not that

I'm complaining. My point is just that they could have saved on the animation budget by doubling up on dwarves. Dopey always seemed pretty happy, Sneezy would have had a good excuse to be grumpy, and if Bashful had been more sleepy, he could been the dwarven Brian Wilson. Or maybe they should have just had one named Bipolar Hypochondriac and called it *Snow White and a Dwarf.* Catchy! **C–**

Bashful

Bashful of what? He sleeps in a single room with six other guys he's known for a couple centuries, if I know my fantasy dwarf life spans. You'd think in that time he'd have managed to loosen up a little. Sure, I can see how having a virgin princess move in would make him a bit tongue-tied with pent-up ardor, but he already *had* the name. **D**

Dopey

Dopey is the only bald, beardless, mute dwarf in the bunch. I'm not sure what that indicates. Maybe he's the dwarf equivalent of a toddler, in which case they're kind of jumping to label the guy, or maybe it's some sort of disorder in his animated chromosomes, in which case the name Dopey is kind of callous but rolls off the tongue better than Developmentally Disabledy. **B–**

Sneezy

At this point I have to wonder how the whole dwarf-naming process goes. Was Sneezy called Sneezy from birth, or was he known as Wrinkled Diaper-Filler until his personal quirk became evident? If he started taking steroid inhalants for his allergies, would he have to change his name to Healthy or would he bear the traces of his former affliction forever? **C**

Sleepy

I sympathize with Sleepy. I enjoy the sleep. I expect he had the weightiest cross to bear of all his, um, brothers? Cousins? Kin. It's hard enough being sleepy, but being a sleepy miner must be a really tough gig. Not only do you have to get up early and work hard, but if you hit a pocket of poison gas, everyone will just think you're passed out on the job again. I'm surprised he lived through the picture. **A**

ARCHIE COMICS CHARACTERS

Archie

The central cultural lesson of Archie is that armless letterman sweaters are never ever going to come back in style. Whether Betty and Veronica are wearing butt-constricting designer jeans or logo-encrusted baby-doll shirts, Archie seems to always have a fondness for that sweater and he always looks like a dork. In fact, in a world where bell-bottoms have been popular twice in the past forty years, the only explanation for the continuing dorkiness of the armless letterman sweater is that Archie comics have a negative influence on fashion. Same with Jughead's beanie. **C–**

Moose

Apparently, you can't be a big dumb guy without a one-syllable mammalian nickname like Moose, Ape, Bear, Bull, or Hoss. Are you a big dumb guy looking for a nickname to call your own? The following are still available: Elk, Gnu, and Whale, or, if you're not too picky, Vole, Mole, and Hare. **C–**

Jughead

I remember some socially aware Archie comic from the eighties in which a DEA agent thought he had Jughead pegged as a drug offender because Juggie never opens his eyes. Is this some sort of druggie trick I don't know about? "Perhaps if I keep my eyes closed, he won't notice that I am high like the weather balloon." Anyhow, this is distracting me from my main question, which concerns the fact that Jughead and Mike Doonesbury share very similar noses and eyelids. To wit: the hell? **B**

Betty

I've never understood the relationship between Betty and Veronica. They appear to enjoy each other's company and to mutually admire their ability to make fashions designed by twelve-year-olds look good, but they're also constantly trying to screw each other over on the Archie front. If that's what dating's all about, I'm glad none of my relationships got started in a "Choc'lit Shop." **B–**

Veronica

If she's so rich and snobby, why isn't she in a private school? You'd think her parents would have pulled her out of Riverdale High about the time DEA agents started hanging around. It's interesting how often rich people are the bad guys in these sorts of comics. Sure, Richie Rich was a nice guy, but all of his cousins were wealthy dickweeds. The only comic I can think of where a rich good guy faces off against the underclass is Batman. **C+**

Reggie

Reggie's an asshole, but he's kind of a boring asshole. He doesn't try to steal Archie's women or anything, he just seems to be comfortable with his assholism and willing to work with it, in spite of usually ending up having to serve as Mrs. Grundy's thong-wearing houseboy as punishment. **D**

QUIZ:
IS THAT PORN
OR EROTICA?

Yes No

☐ ☐ 1. Does the story have two or more consecutive paragraphs describing someone's hands?

☐ ☐ 2. Are genitalia routinely referred to as "the sex"? As in, "He pressed his hard sex against her soft sex and they had sex."

☐ ☐ 3. Are female breasts at any point called by a name with one or more double O's? Examples: "boobs," "gazoongas," "wahoolazooboos."

☐ ☐ 4. Do women in the story apparently achieve orgasm primarily by chanting the word "harder"?

☐ ☐ 5. Is menstruation referred to in any context, ever?

☐ ☐ 6. Does the story make reference to classical mythology? The phrase "oh, God" does not count.

☐ ☐ 7. Does the plot revolve around the seduction of anyone in the landscaping, home repair, or nursing profession?

☐ ☐ 8. Does the story contain any of the following words: "languid," "age-old," "melancholy," or "madcap"?

☐ ☐ 9. Is the title of the story "The [Location of Sexual Activity]"? Examples: "The Cabin," "The Veranda," "The Bahamas."

☐ ☐ 10. Is the main character already naked when the story begins?

☐ ☐ 11. Does the story involve four or more people having sex simultaneously, not strictly in pairs?

☐ ☐ 12. Is anything described as "crotchless"?

Score one porn point for answering "yes" to 3, 4, 7, 10, 11, or 12. Score one erotica point if you answered "yes" to 1, 2, 5, 6, 8, or 9.

More porn points:
    You, my friend, are dealing with what experts in such matters call "porn."
More erotica points:
    What you have there is erotica. It goes well with herbal tea and equally herbal bubble baths.
Tie:
    The tiebreaker is this: If it's in something calling itself an "anthology," it's erotica. Otherwise, welcome to porn.

BASEBALL POSITIONS

Pitcher

In spite of having no other opinions about the rules of baseball, I'm against the designated hitter because I think sports are more interesting when one of the players has to do something at which he sucks. I also think kickers in football should have to be quarterbacks for a couple plays per game and professional golfers should let one of their holes be played by the guy who rakes the sand traps. Anyhow, pitchers are neat because they get to put their arms in ice. **A–**

Catcher

Being a catcher is the only squatting-oriented career I'm willing to picture in my mind. Catchers get to do all the cool stuff like suggest to the pitcher what to throw, tag people out at the plate, and especially rip their face mask off. If I were a catcher, I'd rip my face mask off all the time. I'd probably wear a face mask even while batting so that I could rip it off if I hit a home run or a high foul. **B**

Fielder

I'm sure there are complex differences in the skills required of different fielders, but I don't think I'd retain them if you told me. I think being a fielder would be a largely thankless job; any errors you make look really stupid, and most of your appearances on highlight reels involve you running into walls. **D**

Shortstop

I understand that the position of shortstop is vitally important and requires great skill, but it really messes up the symmetry of the field when someone's on second base. If only the metric system had taken hold in this country, we'd have ten players on a team and everything would even out. Anyhow, if you're a shortstop, you can at least take solace in the fact that your life will never lack for grounders. **C**

Second Baseman

If I were a second baseman, my big thrill would be when the runner gets stuck between me and the first baseman, and we'd get to do that thing where we toss the ball back and forth to catch the guy, or as veteran ballplayers call it, play "Satan's Keepaway." My second big thrill would be tagging the feet of sliding guys, and my third big thrill would be when you get a new jockstrap for the play-offs. **C–**

CARD SUITS

Spades

Spades are supposed to be the evil, unpleasant suit. The ace of spades is the death card for those who won't shell out for a tarot deck, the queen of spades is bad news in hearts, and so forth. But when you think about it, the idea of a suit of cards being evil is kind of strange. It's like looking at your stick shift and saying "Third gear is the *evil* gear!" **C**

Hearts

You have to give hearts credit for being both correctly shaped and colored for their name, albeit in an abstract Valentiney sort of way. And I think it's just as well. I, for one, find it hard to work out tactical strategies while staring at graphic representations of human organs, which is why I suck at competitive surgery. **C+**

Clubs

Clubs are obviously clovers. Or possibly pawnshop symbols. They do not, however, look like clubs, either in the "gentleman's" sense, the "blunt instrument" sense, or the "turkey and ham" sense. I suppose you could draw some parallel between the symbol and the ear hats on the Mickey Mouse Club, but if that was the origin, I'm sure Disney's competent and undead lawyers would have put the kibosh on that years ago. **C−**

Diamonds

I could pick nits with the choice of color, but picking nits could lead to renaming them "rhombuses," which would be bad because, well, it'd be pretty cool, actually. I enjoy the silent "h," and it would make elementary geometry that much easier. Rhombuses it is! Or parallelograms. Either's cool with me. **B**

SOY THINGS

Soy Sauce

You know what I don't get? Low-salt soy sauce. Isn't that like making low-salt salt? The entire purpose of soy sauce is to make things more salty, so why not just use less? My next invention: low-pork pork ribs. **A**

Edamame

These are, if not the bomb, at least the pipe bomb. They're soybeans, salted and in the pod, and they combine the tastiness of peanuts with the fun of peanuts. And they give you something to do while waiting for your sushi to be sculpted. **A**

Tofu

Tofu has come to stand, in this country, for "gross food eaten primarily by masochistic new-agers," but contrary to popular belief, tofu only tastes gross if you can taste it. When cut into tiny pieces and drenched in some other flavor, it merely feels gross! And it's an excellent source of protein and sliminess. **C–**

Natto

To be truly objective and unbiased, I should probably actually taste this. But natto is a fermented soybean dish and if

I liked it, I'd have to question far too many assumptions I have about myself. I might have to try karaoke or humility—presumably not at the same time—and I'm just not prepared for that. **D**

Soy Milk

Another entry in the Hall of Food that Tries to Sound Tastier by Borrowing the Name of Another Food, like meatless "burgers," carob "brownies," and continental "breakfasts." If I ever become a vegan, I think I'll just stick to delicious, cruelty-free Mr Pibb. **D**

DOG TOYS

Food Block

You stick kibble into this big plastic cube with little holes, and the dog has to nose it around a bunch to get the food to fall out. This is intended to be diverting for bored and stupid dogs. So I tried it on myself with some Corn Bugles, using only my nose and feet to get them out, but the experiment was interrupted when someone walked in. **C**

Growly Pull Rag

My favorite part of this game is the growling, both on my part and the dog's. I feel as if for a moment we can truly communicate, that we are linked by one thought: "Let go of the damn rag." It's also a great way to get your dog's score on the Canine Aggressiveness Scale, which is equal to five minus the fingers you have left afterward. **A**

Rawhide Bone

I'm not sure this qualifies as a dog "toy" so much as "an object of fierce territorial devotion." One of the great things about rawhide bones is that they come in so many different sizes, from the eensy Chihuahua model to the massive ones that seem designed for some variety of carnivorous bison. **B**

Frisbee

Sure, this is great if you have one of those leaping-into-the-air sorts of dogs. Most dogs I've encountered have figured out that, lacking legs, Frisbees are unlikely to make a break for it once they hit turf. These dogs are happy to avoid the danger of eye injury or exertion by trotting after the thing once it stops moving. These dogs are usually the same ones that consider "fetch the Frisbee" to be an inferior game to "grab the Frisbee and chew on it until the edges resemble some sort of half-assed, drool-covered lace pattern." **C+**

Dried Pig Ears

A huge pile of dried pig ears may sound like a roadside attraction in one of the more boring states, but they're actually a mainstay of pet-supply chain stores. Nearly all dog toys, from sticks to balls to rubber models of pre-Columbian Inca idols, are just chew toys with varying levels of expense and aerodynamics, but dried pig ears have to be one of the more disturbing chew toys out there. Not only is there the dried aspect, there's also the pig ear aspect. **C−**

VAMPIRE WEAKNESSES

Garlic

As a food, garlic gets an A+, but as the Achilles' heel of bloodsucking undead predators, I dunno. It seems like an insult gone awry: "Gee, Hans, I don't know how we're going to stop this 'vampire' of yours. Have you tried breathing on it?" If vampires had been invented in our era, they might have been repelled by cell phones in restaurants or people who recite the entire plots of TV shows at parties. **D+**

Sunlight

In the novel *Dracula*, sunlight doesn't kill the title vamp, he's just tired and listless during the day, which also applies to half the people I've worked with. Now, of course, this has evolved into current visions of spontaneous inhuman combustion in sunlight or at tanning salons. Which is, to be fair, much cooler. **A**

Crucifixes

My main question is whether alternative cross-shaped items like railroad crossing signs or the American Lung Association logo would work. I've heard revisionist vampire tales in which it's not the cross but the faith that does the work, and that anything that one considers sacred and awe-inspiring would work, which is why I carry a picture of Bjork with me at all times. **C**

Running Water

Beware my Slip 'n Slide, fanged demon! The idea that vampires can't cross running water has largely been ignored in contemporary vampire literature because of the dumbness. The image of a vampire pacing the opposite bank of a river, fuming like Yosemite Sam because he can't get to you, doesn't fit the current psychoerotic take on filmdom's most dapper monster. **D**

Stakes

The method of making the undead dead varies widely, assuming "dump him in a sunny meadow" isn't an option. In some milieu, a stake through the heart does the trick, while in others you have to stake the bloodsucker, chop his head off, stuff his mouth with garlic, and—on the Food Network—bake him at 350 degrees for forty-five minutes. Serves six. Calories per serving: 460. Calories from evil: 250. **B**

FLINTSTONES CHARACTERS

Wilma

It's interesting that nearly all adult male prehistoric people are approximately the shape and proportions of office wastepaper baskets, while the adult females—the ostensibly attractive ones, at least—are wasp waisted, large breasted, and inclined to show more shoulder than is proper before five P.M. or the late Cretaceous era. This is actually supported by the fossil record. (*American Journal of Aesthetic Anthropology*, vol. 24, pp. 34–42, "Secondary Sexual Characteristics in Early Hominids: Do Those Legs Go All the Way Up?") **C**

Fred

Fred Flintstone is an everyman character, which in television shows means "big dumb father figure inclined in roughly equal proportions to fits of unwarranted temper, unqualified ego, and shameless sentimentality." While not up to, say, the Homer Simpson standard, Fred at least outshines the George Jetsons and Father Berenstein Bears of the world by virtue of the fact that he eats towering installations of brontosaurus ribs. **C+**

Barney

I don't think I'd like to live in the *Flintstones* world, if only because the idea of shaving with a clamshell full of stinging insects is off-putting, but if I were forced to be a face right out of history, I'd like to be Barney. He seems like a nice guy, his wife's cute, and he drives a sort of prehistoric Kharmann Ghia. It might get old playing Boo-Boo to Fred's Yogi, but at least I could take solace in the fact that my infant son could snap Fred's neck like fresh celery if it came to that. **B+**

Betty

She may have lacked Wilma's leadership skills, but at least she didn't wear a femur in her hair. I'm not sure where she tracked down a blue animal to skin for her outfit, but it looks good on her. I even find the giggle acceptable, but I recognize that there's room for disagreement and/or a slow slide into psychosis there. However, every time I hear her and Wilma make that "charge it" pun, I want to smash my television, possibly injuring the wisecracking monkey inside. **B−**

Dino

In the first episode with Dino, he can talk. Honest. He sounds like a cross between a snooty waiter and Snagglepuss. At the end of the episode, he joins the family and from then on, it's nothing but yipe yipe yipe. Perhaps it's standard practice to lobotomize one's pets along with spaying or neutering them. Or maybe Dino's playing it canny and plotting his feral revenge. **C−**

QUIZ:
CHRISTIAN METAL BAND
OR *STAR TREK: THE NEXT*
GENERATION EPISODE?

Metal	Trek	
☐	☐	Divine Right
☐	☐	Redemption
☐	☐	Heart of Glory
☐	☐	Edge of Forever
☐	☐	Deliverance
☐	☐	Vengeance Rising
☐	☐	Legacy
☐	☐	Angel One
☐	☐	Peacemaker
☐	☐	The Survivors
☐	☐	Guardian
☐	☐	Homeward

ANSWERS:

Praisers:
   Divine Right, Edge of Forever, Deliverance, Vengeance
   Rising, Peacemakers, Guardian
Phasers:
   Redemption, Heart of Glory, Legacy, Angel One,
   The Survivors, Homeward

Give yourself one point for each correct answer.

0–4 points: You are as Judas or Wesley.
5–8 points: You are as Peter or Guinan.
9–11 points: You are as John or Data.
12 points: You are Christlike and/or Picardian.

THE LEGION OF DOOM

Lex Luthor

The archest of arch-nemeses, so diabolical that he can make even Superman have to sit down and try to figure things out every once in a while. A man this twisted must have a truly dark and smoldering motive, such as, oh, say, baldness. That's right, the Super Friends-era Lex got his start on the road to doom because Superman accidentally made all his hair fall out when he was a kid. This led L.L. to invent giant robots and all sorts of beam-based weaponry but not, for some inexplicable reason, Rogaine. Twenty minutes working on his actual problem instead of yet another half-assed Kryptonite delivery system could have saved a lot of tsuris. **C+**

Sinestro

Sinestro was, in essence, Green Lantern with magenta skin and a huge forehead. I've often figured that my own arch-enemy is probably just me with magenta skin and a huge forehead and that he's probably off having a beer and watching *The Powerpuff Girls*, because that's what I like to do no matter what size my forehead is. But this isn't about me. Sinestro had a yellow power ring, which I always assumed had a weakness to green because that would make sense. But apparently that's not true, and once again my hope for a rational universe is dashed on the rocks of crappy cel animation. **C**

Gorilla Grodd

He's an evil gorilla, but someone named Gorilla Grodd who's a member of the Legion of Doom has no business being anything else. He's the arch-enemy of the Flash. The nemesis of the fastest man on earth is a talking gorilla. That's really random. He's not a particularly fast gorilla or a gorilla with power over the flow of time, he's just a really strong talking gorilla with a bug up his ass. **C–**

Bizarro

How can you not like Bizarro? Him do the opposite of normal people! Him only able to order Egg McMuffin *after* 10:30 A.M.! Him criticize iMac for having *too many* floppy drives! I only wish there were Bizarro versions of everyone, starting with Bizarro Bob Barker, who would end *The Price Am Wrong* by saying "Remember, everyone, let your pets fuck all they want!" **A**

Cheetah

What do you do when you have a scantily clad Amazon with high-heel boots and a "magic rope" in your television show? Why, make her fight a woman in a skintight kitty outfit, of course! It's a show that the kids can enjoy because of the cartoony action and Dad can enjoy because he's a big ol' pervert! If there isn't an episode that climaxes in a vat of baby oil, I'm sad. **B+**

Black Manta

So of course Aquaman's worst enemy is a guy with underwater powers, because if Aquaman's worst enemy had, say, highway overpass powers, it wouldn't be much of a show. "Dr. Turnpike has snarled traffic again? What am I supposed to do, tell a couple of giant squid to crawl to Ohio and stop him? Call me if there's a tidal wave or something." I'm good with tidal waves. Did you know that the Japanese call them 'tsunami'?" **D+**

JAPANESE SNACK FOODS

Pocky

These are little cookie-like sticks dipped in chocolate. Very straightforward and more addictive than "Ben and Jerry's Crack 'n Tobacco Crunch." They also have Melon Pocky, Coconut Pocky, Giant Pocky, some sort of crunchy Pocky, which I think has toffee or something, and Men's Pocky. I'm not sure if those last ones have testosterone in them or just look good with a suit and tie, but there's a certain macho appeal to eating a *man's* chocolate-covered cookie snack. **A+**

Everyburgers

Certainly there's no dearth of food shaped like other food in Western culture—I had a Jell-O salad shaped like a pig just last week—but Everyburger deserves big hand claps for attention to detail. The darned things look unnervingly like hamburgers. The chocolate "meat" is precisely the correct color, and the cookie "bun" actually has minuscule "sesame seeds." If Goldfish Crackers had that much devotion to verisimilitude, they'd all have little glazed eyes staring helplessly up at you. And who wouldn't enjoy that? **A**

Seasoned Cuttlefish Crackers

I don't want to ever hear you say I never ate seasoned cuttlefish crackers for you. They're even shaped like cuttlefish, although I must admit I haven't spent enough time around cuttlefish to tell how precise the likeness is. If you've ever eaten shrimp chips, they taste kind of like those. If you've never eaten shrimp chips, you're probably not going to want to start at this late stage of the game. **C–**

Glico Something or Other

More candy. I picked this one up because it had both a triumphant athlete and a wooden toy duck on the box. Unable to drum up the faintest connection between the two, I bought it. This is a common experience with me and Japanese candy. Anyhow, the wooden toy duck is because the box contains a wooden toy duck, and the triumphant athlete is because the packaging designer was insane. The box also contains weird squishy strawberry candy, kind of like Gummi candy with no will to live. There's just no sports connection whatsoever. **C**

Meiji, Um, Things

I don't know what these are, except that they're vaguely reminiscent of Funyuns. Judging from the packaging, I had assumed they would taste like a happy frog, a hungry little guy with a beard, or a bowl of soup. Upon prying open the bag, however, I was greeted with the familiar aroma of curry and relief. These are quite tasty! They're little crunchy curry units! I can dig it! **B**

Hello Kitty Lips Candy

They don't taste a damn thing like Hello Kitty lips. **D**

SWISS ARMY KNIFE ITEMS

Scissors

These strike me as a bit of a show-off item, packed in there just to show off that innovative Swiss design. ("See? It's sproingy!") They don't look strong enough to cut anything heavier than paper, and I don't hear a lot about people trapped in the woods, forced to clip coupons to survive. But it *is* sproingy. **C**

Leather Awl

Why is this a standard feature? I've never used it, I've never known anybody who used it, and I have no idea why it has a hole in the middle. I'm sure there are people out there who rely on the leather awl to get them through another day of selling cheap bodices to Ren Faire attendees, but they've got to be in the minority. So why the ubiquity of what most people probably think of as the "mystery tool"? **D+**

Bottle Opener

This is handy. I think there are more people out there who use their SAKs to pop open a refreshing, domestically produced brew than use the leather awl, fish scaler, and toothpick combined. I can never find my regular bottle opener, anyway; I think it's built into a spatula or a cheese grater somewhere in my kitchen, but I can never remember where, so this is a great thing to have even at home. **A**

Big Blade

The blade defines a Swiss Army knife. It's right there in the name: "knife." Even if you don't use the blades, without them the tool becomes a "Swiss Army Multifunction Utility Thinger," which lacks panache. At the same time, the blade unnerves me. It doesn't lock in place, and it closes with such a resolute snap that I don't think I've ever put the blade away without the Stephen King lobe of my overacting mind picturing my poor, unprotected finger trapped like a chicken neck under a hatchet. Maybe that's why they make them out of stainless steel. **B+**

Corkscrew

I love this. It's so European. I picture a survivalist somme-lier, living off the land, with only a bold yet elegant Bordeaux and maybe a light Chardonnay to keep body and spirit together. And it makes picnics so picnicky. **A**

Toothpick

This seems like padding. "What the hell, let's tuck a shard of plastic into the case and call it a toothpick. Now we can say it has ten different functions without having to count 'ballast.' " It's not like it's tough to improvise a toothpick from natural materials, if you're not fastidious. And if you are fastidious, you're probably not going to be too big on the idea of a reusable toothpick that's been hanging out in some-one's pocket, no matter how neatly tucked away it is. **C−**

CHICKEN PARTS

Drumsticks

There's a certain finger-licking appeal to any food with a carrying handle. You can wave it around like a deep-fried magic wand, you can use it as a pointing device during lunchtime presentations, and you can pretend you're some sort of barbarian commander who wouldn't know what a fork was if it frothed his omelet. **A**

Wings

Wings are an awful lot of work. Not Alaskan pipeline level work, to be fair, but more than I want to undertake at a picnic. The meat is wedged in among bone, cartilage, tendon, and other icky bits you had to identify in first-year biology. Only for those with nimble teeth and considerable patience. **C–**

Breasts

These are always a good source of amusement for those who consider Uranus puns to be highbrow college boy humor. So much so, in fact, that when I worked at Kentucky Oil-Soaked Chicken during my salad days, we were informed that they were to be called "keels." Keels? **B**

Thighs

People who prefer dark meat are in luck, because thighs are a hefty chuck of meat in easily portable form. There isn't the same landgrab for them that the white-meat bird sections inspire, so you're free to sit back and try not to think about the disturbing notion of chicken thighs. **C**

Giblets

I've never eaten actual giblets, although I have appreciated plenty of giblet-infused gravy. The thing I like about giblets is that they come in their own little bag, and that the bag is stuffed inside the chicken itself, as if the poultry commission wanted you to think that the birds were raised with sanitary little giblet sacs inside of them. Here's the big bummer, though: The giblets you receive aren't actually from the bird in which you receive them! That somehow seems unfair and unkind to both the consumer and the dead bird. **C**

URBAN LEGENDS

Mexican "Dog" Turns Out to Be Hairless Rat

I'll be the first to admit a vague resemblance between Chihuahuas and hairless gutter vermin, but it's a bit beyond suspension of disbelief to imagine that a ditzy old woman would actually mistake the latter for the former. And even if she did, wouldn't one of her friends set her straight? Or is carrying around an obese diseased rodent the sort of thing one politely overlooks in high society, kind of like a crawling, scaly version of spinach in your teeth? **C–**

. . . And on the Door Handle Was a Hook!

Scary, but you'd think that any prospective murderer would make life easier on himself and open the door with the hand that can actually grip things. I've never tried opening a car door with a hook, but one imagines it's something like trying to remove a bra with a spoon. **C**

Girl Accidentally Breeds Spiders in Hair

A classic urban legend, but these days it's not much of a cautionary tale, given that young women rarely wear elaborate beehives any more. "Spiders in the Sanrio Lunchbox" might be more appropriate, but too far from the scalp. Perhaps a paranoid rumor about the dangers of scabies resting in navel piercings is in order. **C+**

Your Kidneys May Be Stolen from Your Body

This is a wonderful horror story, replete with nice improbable touches like waking up naked and bleeding in a bathtub full of ice: I may never eat shrimp cocktail again. The special touch, though, is the humanitarian nature of this legend: It teaches that we, too, can help those in need, if only by being drugged and subjected to nonconsensual and life-threatening surgery. **A**

The Vanishing Hitchhiker

This lacks a certain something. At least the version in *Pee-wee's Big Adventure* had a squiggly Claymation horror face. The usual version just ends with the driver being informed that he gave a lift to a ghost. At least a ghost won't change your radio station or leave hemp seeds all over your upholstery. **D+**

VCR BUTTONS

Eject

It's pretty rare to find eject on a remote control, and that bothers me. I can understand the reasoning: You're going to have to extract your ass from the dents in the couch cushions to grab the tape, anyway, so what do you need an eject button for? And that would make perfect sense except that the front panels of VCRs are inevitably tastefully illegible, requiring you to bend down and get so close to the buttons that you might as well press them with your nose. **B+**

Pause

Pausing your favorite shows and movies is half the reason for buying a VCR. It really shows those tapes who's in charge here. Whatever Nicolas Cage is going off about, he's just going to have to zip it and wait while you grab another Fresca. It's also handy for investigating rumors of on-screen suicides and playing "Is That a Body Double?" **A–**

Rewind

Current rewinding technology is perfectly adequate, but I'm waiting for the VCR that provides distortion-free 1:1 speed visual rewind, also known as "playing the movie backward." Who doesn't like seeing movies run backward? Milk squirts back into people's mouths! Cars pull themselves off lampposts and miraculously repair themselves while smoke pours back into the tailpipe! Disney heroes renounce their loved ones, lose their faith in themselves, and return to their oppressive origins! **C**

Fast Forward

Fast forward is handy for skipping past commercials in recorded TV shows, but more often than not I'll fail to recognize the last commerial in the pack and hit play too late, missing the first few words in the description of the llama-fat-and-summer-melon bisque on *Iron Chef.* I propose the addition of a "fast-forward, but back up a skosh afterward" button. Also, I propose the elimination of fast-forward modes that are too staticky to tell whether you're still on last week's *ER* or you've moved to an old recording of *SeaQuest DSV.* **C–**

Play

Classic in its simplicity, "Play" takes its place along such timeless buttons as "On," "OK," and "Toast." Some may claim that "Play" is too naive for a complex postmodern, precontemporary, meta-historical world where buttons like "Standby" and "Zero Back" hold sway. However, without beacons of selection like "Play," we sink into a quagmire where "control" is relative and we are most "remote" from our own souls. **A**

OFFICE SUPPLIES

Paper Clips

The paper clip was invented nearly a century ago. Since then, there have been all sorts of pretenders to the paper clip throne; plastic triangle clips, Garfield-shaped clips, little tiny binder clips. And yet none of them are any true threat to the ascendancy of the lowly metal paper clip, and for an obvious reason: You can't make bendy shapes out of them. The ability to make bendy shapes at work is intrinsic to the functioning of high-powered American businesspersons everywhere; whether animals, sproingy jumping things, or just abstract expressionist sculpture, bendy paper clip shapes are what hold this country together. **A**

Ballpoint Pens

Most offices are smart enough not to stock the really good pens. They know that you can give away coffee, pads of paper, floppy disks, and even low-end computer systems, but the minute you start to stock nice rollerball pens in an unlocked cabinet, they'll march on out of there at a rate that would bring the strongest corporation to its metaphorical knees. Valuable stock has fallen precipitously on the mere *rumor* that a company is about to start stocking good pens. So instead, you get crappy, blotchy, smeary ballpoints in black, red, and—if you work for a really off-beat, feel-good company—blue. **D+**

White-Out

White-out is not quite as important around the office as it used to be—who uses a typewriter anymore?—but it's still symbolically vital. It's common knowledge that the mother of former Monkee Mike Nesmith became very wealthy as a result of inventing and patenting the formula for white-out. It just goes to show that anyone in this country can, with sufficient ingenuity and a go-get-it spirit, make it rich *and* give birth to a pop star. And isn't that what we all aspire to? **B**

Graph Paper

Some people like your standard 8.5 × 11 ruled paper. Others prefer yellow legal paper for its extra doodle space. Me, I like graph paper. It's great for your basic writing, making it easy to line up indents in a snappy manner; it's great for graphs, of course, and I graph things for the heck of it more often than I care to admit; and it's really great for doodling along the lines to see what things would have looked like on a late-seventies video game system. And there's always the pleasure of impromptu Battleship. **B+**

Binders

I can see why people might like binders; I prefer unruly stacks. Binders remind me too much of junior high, to begin with, and a lot of them seem like they could take off a couple fingers if you closed the loops the wrong way. At least in junior high you had your choice of overexposed media characters and/or unnecessarily enthusiastic sports slogans on your binder. At the office you generally get a couple of dark shades of conventional. **C–**

Staple Removers

Yet another entry in the fun-but-not-for-what-it's-meant-for race. I think I've used a staple remover to remove actual staples maybe twice in my life. I generally just rip the sheets right off the stack; I'm heartless that way. But I love staple removers, anyway, because they represent one of the few times in life that your employer will supply you with a working hand puppet. Don't get me wrong; I don't sit and talk out loud to my staple remover. No, I just silently *pretend* it's talking. Or sometimes I use it to threaten the phone. **A+**

QUIZ: HOW DOES THAT SONG GO?

1. Dee dee *dum* do da *dee* dum *doo* da
   - ☐ "Raspberry Beret," Prince
   - ☐ "Close (To the Edit)," The Art of Noise
   - ☐ "Dee Dee Dum Do Da Dee Dum Doo Da,"
     Dum Do Da

2. Boo boo *wheeeeeeeeyayayayaya*
   whoodoowoodoowoodoo . . . *yang*
   - ☐ "Beat It" guitar solo, Michael Jackson
   - ☐ "Whiskeyclone, Hotel City 1997" intro, Beck
   - ☐ George Clinton, random screaming between sets

3. Womp womp womp *wah wah*, womp womp womp
   waaaaah waaaaaah
   - ☐ "Star Wars Theme"
   - ☐ "Star Wars Theme" (disco remix)
   - ☐ The sound of beating up someone who insists on
     singing the "Star Wars Theme" in public

4. Ooooh, oooh yeah, ooooh
   - ☐ "Violence," Pet Shop Boys
   - ☐ "Shambala," Three Dog Night
   - ☐ Everything Tori Amos has ever recorded

5. Something something *something*, something
   *some*thing baby something
   ☐ Go away
   ☐ Leave me alone
   ☐ Oh, God, it hurts

6. La la la la la la
   ☐ "Crocodile Rock," Elton John
   ☐ "Do-Re-Mi," extended dance remix, Julie
     Andrews with Moby
   ☐ A record store employee being led to a psychiatric
     hospital after being asked too many times to
     identify songs from tiny off-key snippets.

SCORING: Give yourself a point for every question
you answer.

0–2 points:	You didn't answer very many questions, if any.
3–5 points:	You answered a few questions but left at least one unanswered.
6 points:	Congratulations! You answered them all!

LIGHTS

Flashlights

Sweet mother of Britney, where would we be without flash-lights? I weep to consider! Think of all the slumber-party ghost stories left unaccented by high-contrast spooky faces! Think of all the episodes of *The X-Files* having to take place in well-lit libraries and shopping malls! And in our sad secular age, so lacking in rituals, how many of us knew that we had reached adulthood the day we figured out that we can't make our own working Bat-Signal? A world without flashlights would be tragically lacking in intrigue and uses for D-cells. **A**

Night-lights

As comforting as a glowing Scooby-Doo can be—and that's mightily comforting—it doesn't do shit for earthquakes, which was my big night terror growing up, and by "growing up" I mean "until I was in college." It's a side effect of living in California. Anyhow, in '89 I was in a big massive headline-grabbing quake, and I survived, so I'm much better about it all. Plus I'm moving to North Carolina, where earthquakes aren't a problem but night-lights only serve to attract fearsome night-flying insects the size of Happy Meal toys. **C–**

The Sun

Personally, I'm against it. It's hot, I don't know if you've noticed that, and if you get too much of it, it makes your nose fall off. Also, it makes life on earth possible, which means that it's ultimately responsible for those "Stacker2.com" commercials. Finally, did you know that the sun contains 99.8 percent of the total mass of the solar system? Fuck that noise! **D+**

Headlights

"Sure," many people say, "headlights give us a place to put the eyes on our cartoon automobiles, but what else are they good for?" Let me tell you, person. Headlights make it possible to drive at night and not kill people, so let's have no more of your scoffing. **B**

Candles

Nothing's quite so romantic as the ever present possibility of dying in a flesh-charring conflagration. When it's dark, and you're alone with the one you love, bodies bathed in the warm glow of dozens of flickering candles, you think about how important it is to find true love before the house burns down. You also think of that one music video. The one with all the candles. **B**

MARSUPIALS

Opossums

North America gets one lousy marsupial, and let's just say it's not going to win any beauty contests. Or even not-ugly contests. And it wouldn't even get past the quals in the Mammal Intelligence Open. I used to be much more impressed with possums before one of those scientific myth-debunking books explained that they don't so much play dead as fall into startled comas. Another pleasant childhood metaphor thrown under the fridge of science to rot. **C–**

Wombats

In "researching" this Rating, I discovered that Yahoo has a category called Individual Wombats. I just think that's something people should know. Anyhow, I'm inclined to like wombat because "wombat" is a great name. It's got a "wom," and a "bat," and an "omba." They're kind of nondescript animals, cute in a generic pudgy mammal way, but their name spelled backward is "tabmow," and that makes all the difference. **A**

Kangaroos

My Austrialian friends have assured me that kangaroos are actually something of an annoying, car-bumping form of huge vermin. I don't care, they go *boing*. It is the only living mammal that, when jumping, actually makes a *boing boing boing* sound. You can hear it from almost a mile away. "Kangaroo," in fact, is aboriginal Australian for "boing." Okay, those are all lies, but I hear it very clearly in my head. **A**

Tasmanian Devils

Warner Brothers has this so tied up, I'm surprised they're not suing order Dasyuromorphia for trademark infringement. So now a whole generation thinks of Tasmanian devils as living buzz saws that strike fear into all other species and like to pose for T-shirts, when actually they're squat carrion-eaters who got run out of Australia by dingos. Dingos! **D**

Koalas

Koala bears only eat one thing, day in and day out. I had the same experience with instant ramen in college, so I can really identify with these prototypical tree huggers. Koalas look cuddly, but I am led to understand that they're actually irritable, solitary beasts who do not want belly rubs. What kind of mocking god created creatures with poofy ears and big black noses that don't want belly rubs? **B**

COCKTAILS

Martini

Ah, the drink of choice for the pseudo-sophisticate who considered Jell-O shots the height of glamour until *Swingers* came out. You can tell the *real* losers because they specify whether they want their Martini shaken or stirred, but they don't bother to ask for name gin. Whatever difference shaking supposedly makes, it's not going to hide the fact that well gin is the most god-awful substance ever to sterilize a cigarette burn. **D+**

Harvey Wallbanger

With most oddly named drinks (Long Slow Comfortable Screw in a Rusty Black Cadillac, José) the name is, shall we say, the best part. Not Harvey, though. A well-made Harvey Wallbanger is like a wampa: strong, cold, and quite capable of knocking you unconscious. I wouldn't recommend the Galliano on its own, though. By itself it's a disconcerting bright yellow, and it smells like licorice jelly beans. But combined with vodka and fresh orange juice, it becomes something truly remarkable. **A**

Cuba Libre

A good choice for those who find all this froufing about with shakers and sword-shaped toothpicks to be distasteful, and who long for the days when strawberry-kiwi wine coolers were considered a sophisticated beverage selection. What is it? It's a rum and Coke. With lime juice. But it *sounds* good. Pronounce it *koo*-bah *lee*-bray and you'll fit right in with your painfully retro palsy-walsys. **B**

Tequila Shooters

The whole shooter craze never did much for me, but a tequila shot done in the classic style—salt, tequila, lime, involuntary neck spasm—is more than a shooter. It's a brief drama, a tragic opera of spirits that fits in the palm of your hand. Pain and passion, sweetness and tears, citrus and sodium and fermented cactus juice. **B+**

Bloody Mary

Delicious when well prepared. And according to federal school lunch guidelines, it qualifies as a vegetable. One incredibly important note: A Bloody Mary does *not* contain V8. I don't know what kind of blasphemous watercress-infested stew you get by combining V8 and vodka, but a Bloody Mary it isn't. **A**

Mimosa

Mmm . . . *breakfast* booze. It's wonderful how Western culture has produced such a transparent yet socially acceptable method of getting a buzz before noon on Mother's Day. Champagne drinks tend to be a little affected for my tastes, but any port in a storm. As it were. **C**

DOG TRICKS

Stay

Handy if it works. I've heard tell that there are dogs that have been taught to stay even if there's raw meat six feet in front of them. That's got to go against every strand in dog DNA. I'd have imagined that even if you could get the dog's body to stay put, its brain would leap out of its skull, bounce across the lawn, and start gnawing on the steak with its medulla. It just goes to show the power of a charismatic primate. **B+**

Fetch

"Fetch," obviously enough, isn't the trick. The trick is "Having fetched, bring the object back and actually let me have it, rather than turning this into a rousing game of 'hand versus jaw.' " The really cool fetchers are the Frisbee fetchers, the ones that throw themselves up into the air with wild abandon and look like they should be in an ad for some translucent-green citrus sports drink or another. It's a great sport, and yet it's the only one that hasn't been featured on ESPN2 yet. **B**

Play Dead

Isn't this kind of morbid? Outside of heart-wrenching family films, what is the appeal here? Do the people who train their dogs to play dead also teach them tricks like "Fake a bad case of roundworms"? Or is this just the trick that comes free with every dog, given that "Play dead" is basically equivalent to "Lie on the ground and ignore all non-food stimuli"? **D**

Sit

I've known many dogs who are trained to sit given only the subtle physical signal of having their hindquarters grabbed and shoved downward forcefully. The signal for "Lie down" takes two people, and the signal for "Heel" involves waiting patiently for your dog to get bored with whatever it's chasing, sniffing, and/or marking. **C+**

Come

This, like many tricks, is based on the dog's intrinsic faith that food may suddenly become available at any time, so you have to follow up all your leads. Don't get me wrong, I'm sure that the sorts of dogs who trot around the circle at British dog shows do this and other tricks out of fierce loyalty to the alpha mammal, but your average neighborhood-roaming sloppy dog is working on the knowledge that humans produce food at unpredictable intervals. But hey, whatever works. **C**

Speak

This can be kind of fun, although it goes along with "Beg" into the class of "tricks it would be more impressive to teach your dog *not* to do." I've lived next to dogs that had gone way past "Speak" into "Filibuster." **C−**

BABY TOYS

Stacking Doughnuts

I always had a vague sense of disappointment that these weren't actual doughnuts, but what the hell, they're pretty satisfying to gnaw on, anyway. The tapered pole is a little fascist, I should be able to stack them small-to-large if I want, but if that gets too frustrating, they also ricochet in a satisfying manner when thrown. **B–**

Busy Box

Or whatever these things are called. I'm referring to the infant central control panel with the honk button and the spinning barber pole thing and the dial that makes the clicking sound and the crappy hazy mirror, but what do you care, you're a baby, it's not like you need to apply mascara or pimple medicine and the thing that jingles when you spin it. It's a heady experience. I don't know why executives in need of desktop amusement don't just get one of these. I guess it would just be weird to go "Squeek! Squeek! Dammit, Anderson, where are those quarterly reports? Honk! Squeek! Ding!" **A**

Puffy Vinyl Books

I don't know whether this really counts as a toy, but that's why it's waterproof; babies don't discriminate among toys, books, food, and random items that must be pounded on while yelling. So baby items tend to be universally colorful, stain resistant, and reasonably durable. Puffy vinyl books are all of the above, plus they usually have some sort of baby animal theme. **C**

Glowworm

It's this thing you hug and the face glows. That's all well and good, but what happens when the child grows up and needs to learn that it takes more than a hug to make a loved one's face glow? It takes commitment and tolerance and a superhero-esque radiation accident, and these are the values infants these days are sorely lacking. **C–**

Shape-Matching Ball

These are sort of like Perfection without the time limit. If there was a game called Adequacy, it would be like this. I guess circa one year is too early to expect perfection at anything besides drool bubbles, and precious few retain their mastery of those into adulthood. That may be due to a lack of drool-related challenges coming from the minds at Milton Bradley. I may be thinking about this too hard. **C**

PHONE FEATURES

Mute

I can't bring myself to trust mute, no matter how steadfastly the little red light shines. I've been raised on too many sitcoms not to expect mute buttons, microphone off switches, and office door locks to fail whenever it leads to hilarious levels of social awkwardness. It's the same reason I don't dress up in a disguise to make sure my girlfriend isn't cheating on me, only to bungle the attempt and in the process ruin the surprise party she had planned for my birthday. **B–**

Redial

This is another button that can be awkward, because you can hit redial to invite a friend to catch a movie, but you forgot that you tried to call your own mother a half hour ago, and this time she answers the phone, and you end up asking "Who's this?" before realizing what you did, so you can't play it cool and you didn't want to talk to her right now and anyway the movie's going to start real soon so you have to tell your mom you don't want to talk to her or you'll miss the movie and if you're lucky you'll drop into some sort of coma before you get that far. **B**

Emergency Dial

I think I can remember "911" by myself, thanks. Usually, the phone comes with three emergency buttons, and I can't even think of two other numbers that I'd need to call in an emergency situation. I guess I could call the correct time, I always found the time lady's voice kind of soothing, maybe that would help. And I could also call my friend Lindy, because she's never home and has an answering machine, so I could leave cool last words for future generations to treasure. **C+**

Memory Dial

I never use memory dial. This is because I am so lazy that I can't even be bothered to put in the effort to set up effort-conserving devices. Getting memory dial to work would involve working out my phone number priorities in detail, finding the phone instructions, looking up each number in my PDA, hell, it's too tedious to even finish talking about it. Modern phones have life spans so short that, if they were breeding organisms, they'd have to give birth to hundreds of phonelings just to keep the species going, so it just doesn't seem worth it. **C–**

Flash

This is much less exciting than it sounds. Phones could flash in so many interesting ways that it's a pity they use the word to mean "hang up, then stop hanging up real quicklike." I understand this feature is real handy for those with call waiting, but my loathing for call waiting is so great that I consider that a negative, like pointing out that a given dog food can also be used to raise giant infectious death geckos. **C**

Lit Buttons

A great feature, so great that it shouldn't be considered a feature but rather a basic expectation. Since I have to buy a new phone about every six months—I assume this is because about 1983 phone manufacturers started building phone wiring out of atom-thin strands of gossamer moonlight—I sometimes accidentally get one without a lit face, and I am consternated in much the same way that I would be if I bought the one car that didn't have "Comes with a driver's seat!" in the ad. **A**

NINJA WEAPONS

Nunchuks

These were the weapon of choice for misanthropic youths with rich fantasy lives in my junior high. They didn't actually fight with them, of course—that would have involved wonking themselves on the head repeatedly—but they owned a pair. Or more. The reason for this, I suspect, is simply that while hardware stores don't have a "ninja sword" section, they do carry chains, dowels, and black paint. **C–**

Throwing Stars

These combine the mystery of ninja death-dealing with the free wheeling fun of Frisbee, a classic chocolate-and-peanut-butter situation. ("You got Shogun on my Frisbee! You got Frisbee in my Shogun!") They're also great for the movies, because they require no special effects or skill on the part of the thespian-cum-assassin. Shot one: Ninja throws throwing stars. We hear a *thwip thwip thunk thunk* sound. Shot two: Victim has been punctured and/or pinned to the wall by his clothes. It makes *Bewitched* look like a special-effects spectacular by comparison. **A**

Oreo O's

All right, this isn't a ninja weapon. It is, rather, a breakfast cereal. But, I'm not going to be doing another cereal rating for a while, and I wanted to get the word out now. This stuff is just insane. It's mind-cloudingly wonderful. It's a breakfast cereal that tastes just like Oreos! It's uncanny! You pour it in the bowl, you add milk, and boom, you're eating Oreos. It looks a little weird—the O's are dark brown with little flecks of "Stuf," like a film negative of Apple Jacks—but it's just indescribably fantastic. I have a history of falling in love with cereals that get pulled off the market shortly thereafter (Smurfberry Crunch comes to mind), so I advise you to get it while you can, stockpiling it militia-style if necessary. **A+**. Okay, back to the ninjas.

Long Chains with a Hook at the End

This seems a little unnecessarily complicated for ninja, the masters of the "hide, strike, fade into the night" triathlon. Change that to "hide, jump out, throw a chain so that it wraps around your opponent's legs, yank him toward you, poke him with a hook a few times, then fade into the night" and you've lost a lot of the mystique. Add to that the fact that in the movies, characters normally only get the whole chain routine so that the filmmaker can show that the character can defeat even the dreaded chain, which would be impressive except for the fact that the dreaded chain never seems to do much. **D**

Swords

Oh, I'm sure there are all sorts of names for all sorts of swords that your better ninja might be carrying, but they're all ninja swords, and that's what's important. Swords are the second most important aspect of ninja cinema, right after those little footy socks with the big toe in its own little section. You whack them with the sword, then you kick them with the footy sock; it's all part of the plan. **B+**

Smoke Bombs

Okay, I lied. Swords are the *third* most important aspect of ninja cinema. Even with your sword and your footy socks, you just aren't a ninja without your smoke bombs. You can't get in the ninja clubs, you don't get your 10 percent ninja discount at Denny's, and you can't invest pretax income in the ninja 401(k) plan. **A**

ADDED

SPECIAL EXTRA

PAGE-COUNT-PADDING

BONUS

CARTOON SECTION

STARRING LORE

Written and Illustrated by Lore

SIR PHILIP SIDNEY! KUALA LUMPUR!
AN ASSISTANT HYDROGEOLOGIST!

A GOTHIC CATHEDRAL MADE
ENTIRELY OF COCOA PUFFS!

IMPROVISATIONAL
COMEDIANS HATE ME.

LET'S SEE...

WHAT WOULD JESUS ORDER?

THERE ARE MORE THINGS IN
HEAVEN AND EARTH THAN ARE
DREAMT OF IN YOUR PHILOSOPHY.

BECAUSE YOUR PHILOSOPHY SUCKS.

TAKE TWO WHEN ROPIN' AND RIDIN'
OR AS NEEDED WHEN PLUGGED
BY SOME DADGUM VARMINT.

HUH.

WESTERN MEDICINE.

Lore Fitzgerald Sjöberg lives in the San Francisco Bay Area. He edits and writes for the Brunching Shuttlecocks (http://www.brunching.com/), a popular online humor magazine. His hobbies include doubt, ennui, angst, regret, uncertainty, resignation, and puppetry.